DATAOPS FOR BUSINESS

Transform Data into Insights with Agility

Diego Rodrigues

DATAOPS FOR BUSINESS
Transform Data into Insights with Agility

2025 Edition
Author: Diego Rodrigues

Published by StudioD21.

Important Note

The codes and scripts presented in this book are primarily intended to practically illustrate the concepts discussed throughout the chapters. They were developed to demonstrate educational applications in controlled environments and may therefore require adaptation to function correctly in different contexts. It is the reader's responsibility to validate the specific configurations of their development environment before practical implementation.

More than providing ready-made solutions, this book aims to foster a solid understanding of the topics covered, encouraging critical thinking and technical autonomy. The examples presented should be viewed as starting points for readers to develop their own original solutions tailored to the real demands of their careers or projects. True technical competence arises from the ability to internalize essential principles and apply them creatively, strategically, and transformatively.

We therefore encourage each reader to go beyond merely reproducing examples, using this content as a foundation to build scripts and code with their own identity—capable of making a significant impact on their professional journey. This is the essence of applied knowledge: learning deeply to innovate with purpose.

Thank you for your trust, and we wish you a productive and inspiring study journey.

Content reviewed by A.I. with technical supervision.

CONTENTS

GREETINGS

Dear reader,

It is with great enthusiasm that I welcome you on this journey through the world of DataOps for Business. By choosing to explore this topic, you demonstrate not only an interest in deepening your knowledge, but also in acquiring essential skills to transform data into actionable insights with agility and precision. We live in a scenario where data is generated in ever-increasing volumes and where the need for efficiency, automation and governance has never been more critical. This book was written to guide you through the fundamental concepts and best practices of DataOps, an innovative approach that revolutionizes the way companies manage their data.

In this book, you will find not only the necessary theory, but also a practical approach, based on real-world experiences. The goal is to enable you to build efficient data pipelines, automate processes, ensure quality and governance, and integrate DataOps into business strategies. Data management is no longer just a support for operations and has become a competitive differentiator, allowing companies to make faster, smarter and more informed decisions.

DataOps is not just a set of tools or techniques; It is a new way of thinking about the data value chain, from its collection to its strategic use. With large volumes of data come great challenges: ensuring data is reliable, accessible and well-governed requires a structured and collaborative approach. This book offers a complete path from essential fundamentals to the most advanced methodologies, allowing you to master the practices needed to make your organization more efficient and data-driven.

This book is ideal for data professionals, engineers, analysts, technology leaders, and decision makers who want to implement or improve DataOps strategies in their organizations. Throughout the chapters, you will be challenged to understand how to integrate DataOps with artificial intelligence, machine learning, security and compliance, all with a pragmatic approach focused on real results.

As you embark on this reading, you will be guided through topics that range from the fundamental principles of DataOps to its practical application in different industries. We'll explore the best strategies for automation, observability, governance, and scalability, ensuring you're prepared to meet the challenges of the data era. Here, the objective is not just to understand problems, but to apply intelligent and efficient solutions to optimize data flows, reduce waste and maximize the value of information.

Regardless of whether you are a technical professional or a strategic manager, this book serves as a complete guide to help you implement DataOps effectively and in line with your business objectives. The practical approach, accompanied by case studies and consolidated frameworks, ensures that you can immediately apply the concepts learned to your own projects, transforming the way your organization deals with data.

Get ready to explore the most advanced DataOps techniques and tools, from pipeline automation and continuous integration to data orchestration and implementation of security best practices. The journey you are about to begin is full of insights, challenges and, above all, practical solutions that will directly impact your ability to extract value from data.

Enjoy reading and may this book empower you to become a DataOps expert, ready to face the challenges of the future and create solutions that will make a difference in the business world.

Happy reading and success on your journey!

ABOUT THE AUTHOR

Diego Rodrigues

Technical Author and Independent Researcher

ORCID: https://orcid.org/0009-0006-2178-634X

StudioD21 Smart Tech Content & Intell Systems

Email: studiod21portoalegre@gmail.com

LinkedIn: linkedin.com/in/diegoexpertai

International technical author (tech writer) focused on the structured production of applied knowledge. He is the founder of StudioD21 Smart Tech Content & Intell Systems, where he leads the creation of intelligent frameworks and the publication of didactic technical books supported by artificial intelligence, such as the Kali Linux Extreme series, SMARTBOOKS D21, among others.

Holder of 42 international certifications issued by institutions such as IBM, Google, Microsoft, AWS, Cisco, META, Ec-Council, Palo Alto, and Boston University, he works in the fields of Artificial Intelligence, Machine Learning, Data Science, Big Data, Blockchain, Connectivity Technologies, Ethical Hacking, and Threat Intelligence.

Since 2003, he has developed more than 200 technical projects for brands in Brazil, the USA, and Mexico. In 2024, he established himself as one of the leading technical book authors of the new generation, with over 180 titles published in six languages. His work is based on his proprietary TECHWRITE 2.3 applied technical writing protocol, focused on scalability, conceptual precision, and practical applicability in professional environments.

BOOK PRESENTATION

We live in the age of data explosion. Every second, companies around the world generate, store and analyze an unprecedented amount of information. However, this exponential growth in data has brought equally complex challenges: how to manage large volumes of information in an agile, efficient and reliable way? How to ensure that this data is accessible for real-time decision making? How to avoid fragmentation and waste of resources in information management?

This is where the Data Ops becomes essential. More than a methodology, DataOps represents a new way of thinking about the data value chain, combining agile practices, automation and collaboration between teams to transform the chaos of raw data into valuable insights for business. Large companies such as Google, Amazon and Netflix have already adopted DataOps strategies to ensure competitive advantage, reducing the time needed to transform data into action. And now, with this book, you will have access to this knowledge in a structured way and applied to your context.

If you want to become a prominent professional in the world of technology and business, master DataOps for Business it is no longer an option—it is a fundamental requirement. With this guide, you will learn how to structure processes, automate data flows and ensure quality and governance, all with a strategic and practical approach.

What You Will Find In This Book

This book was developed to offer a didactic and applied approach to DataOps, covering everything from fundamental concepts to implementation in real scenarios. Throughout the chapters, you will be guided through a logical path, where each section contributes to the construction of solid and applicable knowledge.

Below, we present a summary of each of the chapters so you know exactly what to expect and how each of them will contribute to your DataOps education.

PART 1: DATAOPS FUNDAMENTALS

Chapter 1 – What is DataOps?
In this first chapter, you will understand the essence of DataOps: what it is, where it came from and why it has become a differentiator for companies that want to extract strategic value from their data. We'll explore the differences between DataOps, DevOps, and MLOps, showing how each approach applies to the data lifecycle.

Chapter 2 – DataOps Principles
Here, you will learn about the pillars of DataOps, including automation, quality, governance and collaboration between teams. We'll look at how these principles help companies avoid data silos and increase efficiency in delivering insights.

Chapter 3 – DataOps Architecture
This chapter covers the main components of the DataOps architecture, from data pipelines to orchestration and monitoring systems. You will understand how to structure an efficient and scalable data flow for your organization.

Chapter 4 – DataOps Culture and Mindset
Implementing DataOps goes beyond tools and processes—it requires a shift in mindset. Here, we explore how to create a DataOps culture within companies, promoting collaboration between engineers, analysts and business leaders.

PART 2: PRACTICAL IMPLEMENTATION

Chapter 5 – Building Agile Data Pipelines
You will learn how to build efficient data pipelines, ensuring that information flows automatically and reliably between different systems.

Chapter 6 – DataOps and Cloud Computing
This chapter explores the relationship between DataOps and cloud computing, covering tools such as AWS, Azure, and Google Cloud to optimize data storage and processing.

Chapter 7 – Data Quality and Governance
Data integrity and security are paramount. Here, we'll look at strategies for ensuring regulatory compliance and data quality throughout the pipeline.

Chapter 8 – Automation and Continuous Integration (CI/CD) for Data
You will understand how to apply CI/CD principles to DataOps, ensuring continuous deliveries and avoiding common problems

such as inconsistency and lack of versioning.

Chapter 9 – Observability and Data Monitoring

In this chapter, we will cover best practices for tracking, auditing and monitoring data flow, ensuring process reliability and preventing failures.

PART 3: DATAOPS IN PRACTICE – REAL CASES

Chapter 10 – DataOps for Business Intelligence (BI)

Discover how DataOps can improve reports and dashboards, making Business Intelligence analyzes more efficient and accurate.

Capítulo 11 – DataOps no Big Data e Machine Learning

This chapter explores how DataOps can accelerate the development and deployment of Machine Learning models, ensuring a continuous flow of data to algorithms.

Chapter 12 – DataOps in Finance and Banking

You will see how the financial sector uses DataOps to improve fraud detection, ensure compliance and optimize transactions.

Chapter 13 – DataOps in E-commerce and Marketing

Digital retail companies rely on data to personalize campaigns and improve user experience. Here, we'll look at real-world examples of how DataOps impacts the industry.

Chapter 14 – DataOps for Healthcare and Biotechnology

From electronic health record management to genomic analysis, DataOps is revolutionizing the healthcare industry.

PART 4: FUTURE AND BEST PRACTICES

Chapter 15 – Strategies for DataOps Teams
How to assemble and structure an efficient DataOps team within an organization.

Chapter 16 – Security and Privacy in DataOps
We will cover essential practices to protect sensitive data and comply with regulations such as LGPD and GDPR.

Chapter 17 – Trends and Innovations in DataOps
What innovations are shaping the future of DataOps? We explore topics such as AI, quantum computing and intelligent automation.

Chapter 18 – How to Implement DataOps in Your Company
A practical guide for those who want to start applying DataOps in their organization, including a detailed checklist.

PART 5: CONCLUSION AND REFLECTION

Chapter 19 – Success Stories and Lessons Learned
We will analyze real cases of companies that implemented DataOps and the benefits they obtained.

Chapter 20 – The Future of Data-Driven Decisions

We close with a reflection on the impact of DataOps on the future of corporate decision-making.

Follow Your Learning Journey

Knowledge in DataOps can be the differentiator that will boost your career or transform your company. This book offers a practical and complete guide, combining theory, applications and strategies to help you master this new data management paradigm.

Don't miss the opportunity to become a DataOps expert. Continue reading and get ready to master data with efficiency and innovation!

CHAPTER 1 – WHAT IS DATAOPS?

DataOps is a methodology designed to optimize the delivery and management of data in organizations that rely heavily on agile processes and automation. The concept arose from the need to improve collaboration between data teams, ensure the quality of information and accelerate the generation of actionable insights for the business. By combining principles of agile development, DevOps and data management, DataOps allows companies to operate with greater efficiency and adaptability.

The evolution of data and the exponential growth of information collected by companies led to the need for a structured model that could facilitate the organization and processing of this information. As technologies such as artificial intelligence, machine learning and big data became central to business strategy, it became apparent that traditional data management methods were not sufficient to meet demand.

The first signs of DataOps emerged with the need to integrate software engineering practices into data operations, applying automation, versioning and quality control to the flow of information. The objective is to ensure that data is always available, reliable and ready to be used in decision making.

The DataOps methodology is not limited to a set of specific tools or technologies. It involves a disciplined approach to managing data end-to-end, from collection to delivery for analysis. With well-defined processes, DataOps facilitates integration between different platforms and systems, allowing data to flow efficiently and securely throughout the organization.

Companies that adopt DataOps are able to significantly reduce the time needed to transform data into actionable insights. Furthermore, the methodology helps eliminate operational bottlenecks, promoting a more collaborative environment between data scientists, data engineers and IT teams.

The main difference between DataOps and traditional data management approaches is automation and continuous integration. Instead of relying on time-consuming manual processes, DataOps automates the collection, transformation and delivery of data, ensuring consistency and reliability. This model is based on the agile philosophy, allowing changes to be implemented quickly without compromising data quality.

Differences between DataOps, DevOps and MLOps

Although they share similar concepts, DataOps, DevOps and MLOps have different purposes within the technology ecosystem.

DevOps is a practice aimed at integrating development and operations, focusing on automating the software life cycle. It seeks to reduce the time between writing code and deploying it to production, ensuring that new features are delivered quickly and reliably.

DataOps, on the other hand, applies these same principles to data flow. The main concern is not in software development, but in creating data pipelines that guarantee quality, security and governance. DataOps introduces practices such as data versioning, automated testing and continuous monitoring to ensure that information is always available and up to date.

MLOps is an extension of these practices focused on machine learning. It focuses on automating the lifecycle of machine learning models, from experimentation to production deployment. The goal is to ensure that models are updated regularly and that the data used to train them is reliable and representative.

The table below summarizes the main differences between these methodologies:

Feature	DevOps	Data Ops	MLOps
Main focus	Software development	Data processing and delivery	Machine Learning Models
Automation	CI/CD to code	CI/CD for data pipelines	CI/CD for machine learning models
Quality	Automated software testing	Automated data testing	Model monitoring and retraining
Governance	Code version control	Data versioning	Model version control

Although distinct, these concepts can coexist within an organization. Companies using DataOps often integrate DevOps and MLOps practices to ensure an efficient workflow.

Benefits of DataOps for Business

Adopting DataOps brings significant advantages to companies that rely on data to make strategic decisions. By optimizing the collection, processing and analysis of information, the methodology allows organizations to operate with greater agility and reliability.

One of the main benefits of DataOps is the reduction in the time required to transform data into actionable insights. Companies that rely on traditional processes often face delays in reporting and analysis due to operational bottlenecks. With DataOps, these bottlenecks are eliminated through automation and continuous integration, ensuring data is always available for use.

Another important benefit is the improvement in data quality. DataOps incorporates validation practices and continuous monitoring, ensuring that errors are detected and corrected quickly. This is essential for organizations that rely on accurate information to optimize their operations.

Security and governance are also improved with DataOps. The methodology allows companies to establish strict controls over access and use of data, ensuring compliance with regulations such as LGPD and GDPR. Additionally, data versioning and traceability facilitate internal audits and investigations.

Collaboration between teams is another fundamental aspect of DataOps. In many companies, data scientists, engineers and analysts work in isolation, resulting in information silos. DataOps promotes an integrated approach, allowing different teams to share knowledge and resources efficiently.

The financial impact is also significant. By reducing waste and optimizing infrastructure usage, DataOps allows companies to save resources and increase operational efficiency. This translates into greater return on investment for data-driven projects.

DataOps Implementation

The adoption of DataOps requires cultural and structural changes within companies. The first step is to define an efficient data pipeline, ensuring that all steps — from ingestion to analysis — are automated and monitored.

Choosing suitable tools is also essential. Platforms like Apache Airflow, Kubernetes, and Spark are widely used to orchestrate and process large-scale data. Integration with cloud services such as AWS, Google Cloud and Azure facilitates scalability and infrastructure management.

Implementing automated tests is another crucial aspect. Just like in software development, DataOps requires that data quality be validated continuously. Tools like Great Expectations allow you to create automated tests to ensure information integrity.

Continuous monitoring should also be part of the strategy. Using dashboards and alerts makes it easier to detect anomalies and allows data teams to quickly react to any issues.

Another critical factor is documentation and data versioning. DataOps encourages the use of code repositories to store and manage pipelines, ensuring traceability and control over modifications.

Successful DataOps implementation depends on the involvement of the entire organization. Technology leaders must promote adoption of the methodology and ensure that teams have access to necessary training and resources.

As more companies recognize the importance of DataOps, its adoption is likely to expand rapidly. With well-structured processes and the correct combination of tools, DataOps can transform the way data is managed, making organizations more agile, innovative and competitive.

CHAPTER 2 – DATAOPS PRINCIPLES

Digital transformation has made data an essential asset for companies seeking innovation and competitive advantage. Efficient information collection, processing and analysis processes depend on an agile and well-organized structure. DataOps emerges as a model that combines automation, governance, quality and continuous collaboration to ensure that data flows reliably and quickly between systems.

Companies that adopt DataOps are able to accelerate the delivery of insights, reduce errors, and maintain information integrity without compromising security and regulatory compliance. The fundamental principles of this approach include automation and agility in data management, rigorous quality and governance, and a strong culture of collaboration between teams.

Automation and agility in data management

Automation reduces manual intervention, minimizes errors and ensures that processes run faster and more consistently. Manual workflows result in delays and failures to deliver critical information. With DataOps, tool integration allows you to create data pipelines that automate everything from collection to availability for analysis.

Well-structured pipelines organize the extraction, transformation and loading of data efficiently. Platforms such as Apache Airflow, Prefect and Dagster make it possible to orchestrate these flows, ensuring that each step is executed at the correct time.

Implementing pipelines allows companies to program automated processes for continuous data ingestion. A typical flow involves obtaining information from transactional databases, external APIs, or IoT sensors, followed by processing and storing it in a data lake or data warehouse.

The code below represents an automated pipeline using Apache Airflow to ingest data from a relational database, transform it, and load it into an analysis environment:

python

```
from airflow import DAG
from airflow.operators.python import PythonOperator
from datetime import datetime
import pandas as pd
import sqlalchemy

def extract_data():
    engine = sqlalchemy.create_engine("postgresql://user:password@host/db")
    query = "SELECT * FROM sales_data WHERE date >= CURRENT_DATE - INTERVAL '1 day'"
    df = pd.read_sql(query, engine)
    df.to_csv('/tmp/extracted_data.csv', index=False)

def transform_data():
    df = pd.read_csv('/tmp/extracted_data.csv')
    df['total_price'] = df['quantity'] * df['unit_price']
    df.to_csv('/tmp/transformed_data.csv', index=False)

def load_data():
    engine = sqlalchemy.create_engine("postgresql://user:password@host/analytics_db")
    df = pd.read_csv('/tmp/transformed_data.csv')
    df.to_sql('processed_sales', engine, if_exists='replace', index=False)
```

```
day = DAY(
    'dataops_pipeline',
    schedule_interval='@daily',
    start_date=datetime(2024, 1, 1),
    ketchup=False
)

extract_task = PythonOperator(task_id='extract',
python_callable=extract_data, dag=dag)
transform_task = PythonOperator(task_id='transform',
python_callable=transform_data, dag=dag)
load_task = PythonOperator(task_id='load',
python_callable=load_data, dag=dag)

extract_task >> transform_task >> load_task
```

This flow scheduled to run daily extracts data from a database, performs transformations and loads it into an analysis environment. The modular structure allows each step to be monitored and optimized as needed.

Automation is also present in versioning and controlling changes to data. Tools like DVC (Data Version Control) make it possible to track changes to datasets, ensuring that analyzes and machine learning models are reproducible.

Quality, governance and observability

The quality of the data directly influences the reliability of the insights extracted. An error in the pipeline can compromise financial reports, demand forecasts and strategic decisions. Strict validation practices ensure that only correct and coherent information is used.

Applying automated tests allows you to detect inconsistencies and anomalies before data is made available for analysis. A common approach is to use frameworks like Great Expectations to define automated tests.

python

```python
import great_expectations as ge

df = ge.read_csv("/tmp/transformed_data.csv")

expectation_suite = {
    "expect_column_values_to_be_between": {
        "column": "total_price",
        "min_value": 0,
        "max_value": 10000
    },
    "expect_column_values_to_not_be_null": {
        "column": "customer_id"
    }
}

for expectation, params in expectation_suite.items():
    getattr(df, expectation)(**params)
```

This code checks whether the column values total_price are within an expected range and if customer_id does not contain null values.

Data governance defines rules to ensure compliance with regulatory standards and internal security standards. Companies operating in highly regulated industries, such as finance and healthcare, need to ensure that sensitive information is protected and only accessed by authorized users.

Implementing role-based access control (RBAC) is a common practice. Solutions like AWS IAM, Azure AD, and Apache Ranger allow you to set permissions for users and groups, ensuring that only authorized people can modify or view certain sets of data.

Observability allows you to monitor the health of pipelines and detect problems in real time. Detailed logs and metrics make it easy to identify failures and quickly remediate incidents. Systems like Prometheus and Grafana allow you to visualize pipeline performance and generate alerts for critical events.

Collaboration between data teams

Integration between technical and business teams is fundamental to the success of DataOps. Data scientists, data engineers, and analysts need to share information and work together to ensure data meets organizational needs.

An efficient approach is to adopt collaborative platforms that centralize data and documentation management. Tools such as dbt (Data Build Tool) allow different teams to contribute to the construction and maintenance of data models, ensuring transparency and consistency.

The culture of knowledge sharing is also encouraged through documentation and code versioning. Git repositories store pipelines, scripts, and configurations, allowing any changes to be reviewed and tracked.

Communication between teams is facilitated by the use of agile methodologies, such as Scrum and Kanban. Setting short sprints and daily meetings keeps everyone aligned on project progress and allows you to quickly adapt to changing requirements.

Process standardization and automation reduce dependence on manual tasks, allowing teams to focus on higher value-added activities. CI/CD tools for data ensure that new implementations are tested and validated before deploying to production.

The alignment between technology and business objectives ensures that data is used strategically. Collaboration between different areas of the company allows challenges to be identified and resolved proactively.

The application of DataOps principles results in greater operational efficiency, cost reduction and increased analysis reliability. Companies that adopt these practices gain a clearer view of their data and can make decisions based on accurate, up-to-date information.

CHAPTER 3 – DATAOPS ARCHITECTURE

The DataOps architecture is a structured model that enables the automation, scalability and governance of data processes within an organization. Its goal is to ensure that information flows efficiently, reliably and securely from source to end consumers, reducing the time required to transform raw data into actionable insights.

Implementing DataOps requires a robust infrastructure and well-defined components so that data flows are executed in an automated and continuously monitored manner. This framework is based on three main pillars: data pipelines, orchestration and monitoring.

Essential components: pipelines, orchestration, and monitoring

Data pipelines are automated flows that ensure the movement, transformation and storage of information. A well-designed pipeline allows data to be extracted from different sources, processed, and made available for consumption without manual intervention.

Building pipelines involves defining data sources, processing and final destination. Sources can include relational databases, APIs, CSV files, or streaming systems. Processing may involve transformations, aggregations and validations, while the final destination may be a data warehouse, a reporting system or a machine learning application.

Automating these flows is essential to ensure consistency and scalability. Tools like Apache Airflow and Prefect allow you to define pipelines in a modular way, ensuring that each step can be monitored and automatically restarted in case of failures.

The code below exemplifies a pipeline using Apache Airflow to process sales data and store it in an analysis environment:

python

```python
from airflow import DAG
from airflow.operators.python import PythonOperator
from datetime import datetime
import pandas as pd
import sqlalchemy

def extract_data():
    engine = sqlalchemy.create_engine("mysql://
user:password@host/sales_db")
    query = "SELECT * FROM transactions WHERE date >=
CURDATE() - INTERVAL 1 DAY"
    df = pd.read_sql(query, engine)
    df.to_csv('/tmp/extracted_data.csv', index=False)

def transform_data():
    df = pd.read_csv('/tmp/extracted_data.csv')
    df['total_price'] = df['quantity'] * df['unit_price']
    df.to_csv('/tmp/transformed_data.csv', index=False)

def load_data():
    engine = sqlalchemy.create_engine("postgresql://
user:password@host/analytics_db")
    df = pd.read_csv('/tmp/transformed_data.csv')
    df.to_sql('processed_sales', engine, if_exists='replace',
index=False)

day = DAY(
```

```
    'sales_data_pipeline',
    schedule_interval='@daily',
    start_date=datetime(2024, 1, 1),
    ketchup=False
)

extract_task = PythonOperator(task_id='extract',
python_callable=extract_data, dag=dag)
transform_task = PythonOperator(task_id='transform',
python_callable=transform_data, dag=dag)
load_task = PythonOperator(task_id='load',
python_callable=load_data, dag=dag)

extract_task >> transform_task >> load_task
```

This framework defines an automated workflow for extracting data from a MySQL database, processing it, and storing it in a PostgreSQL analytics database. Code modularity allows you to add new transformations or adjust steps as needed.

Pipeline orchestration ensures that different data processes are executed in the correct order and with well-defined dependencies. Efficiently executing data flows requires a system that can coordinate tasks, set priorities, and manage failures.

Orchestration platforms, such as Apache Airflow, Apache NiFi and Dagster, allow you to schedule and control distributed tasks, ensuring that critical processes are executed at the appropriate time. Integration with cloud computing services enables scalability and flexibility in managing complex workloads.

Continuous monitoring of data pipelines allows you to quickly detect failures and avoid negative impacts on operations. Tracking metrics such as execution time, error rate, and volume of data processed helps identify bottlenecks and optimize workflow performance.

Tools like Prometheus and Grafana are widely used to collect and visualize real-time metrics. Configuring alerts allows technical teams to be automatically notified of failures or degradations in pipeline performance.

Data infrastructure: on-premises vs. cloud

The choice of data infrastructure depends on factors such as data volume, security requirements and operational costs. Companies can choose to store and process their data in on-premise environments, in the cloud or in a hybrid approach.

On-premise environments offer greater control over infrastructure and can be advantageous for companies that deal with highly sensitive data. However, the maintenance and scalability of this type of environment requires significant investments in hardware, licensing and specialized technical staff.

Cloud computing offers flexibility and scalability, allowing companies to increase or reduce their processing capacity according to demand. Providers like AWS, Azure, and Google Cloud offer managed services that simplify the implementation of data pipelines, reducing the need for your own infrastructure.

Adopting hybrid architectures allows organizations to combine the benefits of both models. Critical data can be stored locally to ensure regulatory compliance, while analytical workloads can be processed in the cloud to take advantage of the scalability of managed services.

Core tools and technologies

Implementing DataOps depends on choosing appropriate tools for each stage of the data flow. Several solutions are available to facilitate the automation, orchestration and monitoring of data processes.

For data pipelines, Apache Airflow, Apache NiFi, and Prefect are widely used to define and manage automated workflows. These platforms allow tasks to be scheduled, monitored, and escalated as needed.

Data storage and processing can be optimized with solutions like Snowflake, Google BigQuery, and Amazon Redshift, which offer optimized performance for large-scale analytical queries.

To ensure quality and governance, tools like Great Expectations, dbt, and Apache Atlas allow you to implement automated testing, metadata tracking, and regulatory compliance.

Monitoring and observability are essential for detecting problems and optimizing pipeline performance. Systems like Prometheus, Grafana and Datadog provide detailed metrics and alerts to ensure processes are operating as expected.

The integration of these technologies allows organizations to implement DataOps efficiently, ensuring that data is processed and delivered reliably. The choice of tools must consider scalability, cost and compatibility with the systems already used by the company.

A well-planned DataOps architecture allows data to flow in a structured and secure manner, reducing the time required for analysis and decision making. The combination of automated pipelines, efficient orchestration and continuous monitoring results in a more agile and resilient data environment, capable of meeting the strategic needs of organizations.

CHAPTER 4 – DATAOPS CULTURE AND MINDSET

The adoption of DataOps goes beyond the implementation of tools and methodologies. Real transformation occurs when an organization develops a culture focused on efficiency, collaboration and automation in data management. A DataOps mindset allows teams to work in an integrated manner, eliminating barriers between departments and ensuring that data is treated as a strategic asset.

The DataOps culture emphasizes principles such as continuous collaboration, transparency, incremental improvement, and an agile mindset. The creation of this environment requires structural changes, training of the professionals involved and a commitment to good practices that guarantee efficiency and reliability in the data flow.

How to build a DataOps culture in companies

Companies that want to implement DataOps need to reformulate their internal processes and establish clear guidelines on data processing. Cultural transformation involves technical and organizational aspects, ensuring that the entire team understands the importance of automating and standardizing data flows.

Leadership plays an essential role in creating a DataOps culture. Directors and managers must reinforce the need for a data-driven environment and support initiatives that promote integration between teams. Defining performance metrics and data quality indicators helps demonstrate the benefits of the DataOps approach and encourages buy-in from the professionals involved.

The adoption of DataOps depends on team training. Continuous training in automation, data versioning, monitoring and orchestration technologies allows professionals to act more efficiently and strategically. Internal training programs and access to certifications ensure that employees are prepared to deal with changes in processes.

Implementing standards and best practices accelerates DataOps adoption. The use of governance frameworks and automation tools ensures that processes are replicable and auditable. Data versioning and clear documentation of pipelines are fundamental elements to ensure traceability and regulatory compliance.

Automated workflows and continuous reviews avoid reliance on time-consuming manual processes and reduce the occurrence of errors. Structuring scalable and monitored pipelines allows data to be processed and delivered efficiently, increasing the reliability and availability of information for analysis.

Breaking down silos and

multidisciplinary collaboration

The fragmentation of data teams hinders process efficiency and makes it difficult to deliver valuable insights to the business. The DataOps culture promotes collaboration between data engineers, analysts, data scientists and business professionals, eliminating silos and encouraging information sharing.

Breaking down silos occurs when teams adopt processes and tools that encourage integration. Centralizing data in accessible repositories and using collaborative platforms reduces duplication of efforts and ensures that all areas have access to the same information.

The creation of multidisciplinary teams accelerates the implementation of DataOps. The formation of squads that bring together professionals from different specialties allows solutions to be developed and validated more efficiently. Integration between technical teams and business areas ensures that data is analyzed within the appropriate context and that the insights generated are actionable.

Using versioning and code management tools, such as Git, facilitates collaboration. Storing pipelines in shared repositories allows different teams to contribute to improving processes, ensuring traceability and change control.

Efficient communication is essential for multidisciplinary collaboration. The use of agile methodologies, such as Scrum and Kanban, helps to structure the work of teams and ensure the continuous delivery of improvements to data processes. Frequent alignment meetings and the use of monitoring dashboards allow everyone to track the progress of DataOps initiatives.

Transparency in data management strengthens collaboration. Controlled, well-documented access to data streams reduces reliance on specific knowledge and allows new team members to quickly integrate into operations.

Data lifecycle and agile mindset

DataOps introduces an iterative approach to data management, allowing processes to be continually improved and adjusted as business needs evolve. Applying agile methodologies to data flows ensures that teams can quickly respond to new demands and efficiently correct failures.

The data lifecycle in DataOps follows well-defined steps: collection, ingestion, processing, analysis, availability and continuous monitoring. Each of these phases must be automated and integrated, ensuring that data is delivered with quality and on time.

Automating data collection reduces the time required to make information available for analysis. The implementation of structured pipelines allows data from different sources to be ingested in a standardized way and without manual intervention.

Data processing is optimized through the application of automated transformations and the use of scalable technologies. The implementation of frameworks such as dbt allows the standardization of transformations and the reuse of models, ensuring operational efficiency.

Data is made available quickly, allowing analysts and decision makers to have immediate access to the necessary information. Integration with Business Intelligence platforms and interactive panels facilitates data visualization and interpretation.

Continuous monitoring of data pipelines ensures issues are identified quickly. Configuring alerts and observability dashboards allows technical teams to act proactively to correct errors.

Adopting an agile mindset in data management allows processes to be adjusted incrementally. Small, continuous improvements ensure that workflows evolve with business needs and that data quality is maintained over time.

Structuring an automated testing environment for data reduces risks and ensures that changes to pipelines are validated before being deployed. Tools like Great Expectations make it possible to create tests to check the quality of the information processed.

Incorporating DevOps practices into DataOps strengthens process reliability. The use of continuous integration and continuous deployment (CI/CD) allows new versions of pipelines to be implemented safely and without impact on operations.

The agile mindset applied to DataOps transforms the way companies manage their data. The adoption of short development cycles, constant validation of deliveries and a focus on automation guarantee greater efficiency and reliability in the processing of information.

Creating a DataOps culture requires organizational commitment and structural changes in data management processes. Collaboration between teams, breaking down silos and applying agile methodologies ensure that companies can extract maximum value from their data and make strategic decisions based on reliable information.

CHAPTER 5 – BUILDING AGILE DATA PIPELINES

Building efficient data pipelines is critical to ensuring that information flows in a structured and reliable manner within an organization. Automating flows reduces the time needed to process and deliver insights, minimizes errors and increases systems scalability. The use of modern ETL (Extract, Transform, Load) and ELT (Extract, Load, Transform) techniques allows data to be manipulated in an optimized way, meeting analytical and operational demands.

Implementing well-designed pipelines allows data to be collected, transformed, and uploaded to different destinations without manual intervention. Continuous monitoring and detailed logging ensure that processes are auditable and failures are detected quickly.

Data flow automation

Automating pipelines eliminates the need to manually perform repetitive tasks and reduces the chance of data inconsistencies. The use of orchestration tools allows processes to be chained efficiently, ensuring that each step occurs in the correct order and at the appropriate time.

Platforms such as Apache Airflow, Prefect and Dagster allow the definition of automated workflows that coordinate the execution of different tasks within the pipeline. Configuring dependencies between tasks ensures that no steps are started before prerequisites are completed.

Creating reusable and modular pipelines improves the maintainability and scalability of data processes. Defining isolated tasks allows individual components to be modified or replaced without affecting the entire flow.

Implementing an automated pipeline using Apache Airflow can be done as follows:

python

```python
from airflow import DAG
from airflow.operators.python import PythonOperator
from datetime import datetime
import pandas as pd
import sqlalchemy

def extract_data():
    engine = sqlalchemy.create_engine("postgresql://
user:password@host/db")
    query = "SELECT * FROM sales_data WHERE date >=
CURRENT_DATE - INTERVAL '1 day'"
    df = pd.read_sql(query, engine)
    df.to_csv('/tmp/extracted_data.csv', index=False)

def transform_data():
    df = pd.read_csv('/tmp/extracted_data.csv')
    df['total_price'] = df['quantity'] * df['unit_price']
    df.to_csv('/tmp/transformed_data.csv', index=False)

def load_data():
    engine = sqlalchemy.create_engine("postgresql://
user:password@host/analytics_db")
    df = pd.read_csv('/tmp/transformed_data.csv')
    df.to_sql('processed_sales', engine, if_exists='replace',
index=False)

day = DAY(
```

```
   'dataops_pipeline',
   schedule_interval='@daily',
   start_date=datetime(2024, 1, 1),
   ketchup=False
)

extract_task = PythonOperator(task_id='extract',
python_callable=extract_data, dag=dag)
transform_task = PythonOperator(task_id='transform',
python_callable=transform_data, dag=dag)
load_task = PythonOperator(task_id='load',
python_callable=load_data, dag=dag)

extract_task >> transform_task >> load_task
```

The workflow is structured to extract data from a PostgreSQL database, perform transformations and store it in an analytical environment. Daily execution ensures that new information is processed automatically without the need for human intervention.

Integrating pipelines with cloud services allows data to be processed on a large scale with high availability. Platforms like AWS Step Functions, Google Cloud Dataflow, and Azure Data Factory offer managed solutions for orchestrating complex data flows.

Best practices for efficient ETL/ELT

The choice between ETL and ELT depends on the volume and complexity of the data, as well as the analytical needs of the company. Traditional ETL involves extracting and transforming data before loading it into the target system. ELT reverses this order, loading the raw data before applying transformations within the storage environment itself.

ETL is best suited for scenarios where data needs to be cleaned and structured before storage. It is widely used in relational databases and traditional data warehouses.

ELT is ideal for modern data lake-based architectures where large volumes of raw data are loaded first and transformations are performed on demand. Tools like dbt (Data Build Tool) are often used to perform SQL transformations directly in the data warehouse.

Optimizing transformations ensures that pipelines are efficient and do not overload processing systems. Using partitions and indexing improves query performance by reducing the time needed to extract relevant information.

Validation and data quality are critical to prevent inconsistent information from propagating throughout the pipeline. Applying automated tests before final loading ensures that only correct data is used.

The Great Expectations framework enables the creation of rules to validate data integrity:

python

```
import great_expectations as ge

df = ge.read_csv("/tmp/transformed_data.csv")

expectation_suite = {
    "expect_column_values_to_be_between": {
        "column": "total_price",
        "min_value": 0,
        "max_value": 10000
    },
    "expect_column_values_to_not_be_null": {
        "column": "customer_id"
    }
}

for expectation, params in expectation_suite.items():
```

```
getattr(df, expectation)(**params)
```

Automatic validation prevents erroneous data from being loaded, ensuring greater reliability in the analytical process.

Data monitoring and logging

Continuous monitoring of pipelines is essential to detect failures and optimize performance. Collecting metrics such as execution time, failure rate, and volume of data processed helps identify bottlenecks and predict potential problems.

Detailed logging allows you to track each step of the pipeline and makes debugging easier in case of errors. Tools such as ELK Stack (Elasticsearch, Logstash and Kibana) and Fluentd are used to centralize logs and visualize execution information.

Configuring alerts enables technical teams to be immediately notified of failures or performance degradation. Systems like Prometheus and Grafana offer dashboards for real-time monitoring and configurable alerts.

Auditing pipelines ensures that runs are recorded and any changes to data can be tracked. Data versioning and metadata storage allow you to roll back unwanted changes and ensure regulatory compliance.

Integrating observability practices into DataOps improves process predictability and reduces the time required to resolve incidents. The combination of structured logging, analytical dashboards and automated monitoring strengthens the reliability and scalability of data pipelines.

Building agile pipelines allows organizations to optimize their data processes and make faster, more accurate decisions. The automation of flows, the application of ETL/ELT best practices and the implementation of continuous monitoring guarantee operational efficiency and greater control over information.

CHAPTER 6 – DATAOPS AND CLOUD COMPUTING

The increasing adoption of cloud technologies has significantly transformed the way companies manage, store and process data. With the advent of cloud computing, scalability, flexibility and agility have become fundamental in building efficient data solutions, and DataOps has adapted to these needs. The use of DataOps in cloud environments provides not only greater performance, but also resource optimization and cost reduction. In this chapter, we will explore how scalable cloud architecture and leading cloud tools are applied in the context of DataOps.

Scalable architecture for DataOps in the cloud

Scalability is one of the main advantages of cloud computing, allowing companies to adjust their resources according to demand. In the context of DataOps, this translates into flexibility to handle large volumes of data in real time, without compromising efficiency. The scalable architecture for DataOps in the cloud involves the use of data storage, processing and orchestration solutions that can grow as needed, without interruptions in data flows.

The cloud enables the creation of dynamic data pipelines that can be easily adjusted to handle spikes in demand or load shedding without the need to restructure physical infrastructure. The elasticity offered by leading cloud platforms such as AWS, Azure and GCP allows companies to scale their data operations efficiently, with the ability to add or remove resources as needed.

Furthermore, the concept of "serverless computing" is an important innovation for DataOps, where users can perform data processing functions without the need to manage servers directly. This facilitates the automation and orchestration of data pipelines, as the infrastructure is managed by the cloud platform itself. Instead of worrying about allocating computing resources, data teams can focus on creating and managing data flows.

Cloud tools for DataOps: AWS, Azure, GCP

Each of the major cloud platforms – AWS (Amazon Web Services), Azure (Microsoft) and GCP (Google Cloud Platform) – offers specific tools that can be leveraged to implement DataOps. Each of these tools has its own characteristics, but they all share the goal of automating, scaling, and optimizing data management.

AWS (Amazon Web Services)

At AWS, one of the main tools for DataOps is AWS Data Pipeline, which enables the automation of data flows between different AWS services and external systems. THE AWS Glue, a serverless platform for ETL (Extraction, Transformation and Loading), is another essential tool for DataOps. It facilitates the process of integrating and preparing data for analysis, ensuring that the data is ready to be used in dashboards or machine learning models.

Furthermore, the Amazon S3 is used for storing large volumes of unstructured data, while Amazon Redshift serves as a data warehouse for analyzing large data sets. These tools, together with the Amazon SageMaker for creating and training machine learning models, they offer a robust and scalable infrastructure for DataOps.

Azure (Microsoft)

No Azure, o Azure Data Factory is an essential tool for automating data flows. It allows the creation of pipelines to move and transform data from different sources to different destinations, being highly integrated with other Azure services. THE Azure Databricks, which offers a collaborative environment of notebooks and clusters for large-scale data processing, is also an excellent option for DataOps in cloud environments.

Another important Azure service is Azure Synapse Analytics, which combines big data and data warehousing functionalities, allowing real-time analysis of large volumes of data. This makes it easier to integrate data from multiple sources and build complex pipelines to create valuable insights for the business.

GCP (Google Cloud Platform)

Na GCP, o Cloud Dataflow is a fundamental tool for creating data pipelines. It offers real-time data processing and integration with other GCP tools, such as BigQuery and Cloud Pub/Sub, enables a robust and scalable DataOps implementation. THE BigQuery, as an analytical data warehouse, facilitates the analysis of large data sets quickly and efficiently, while the Cloud Storage offers highly scalable storage solutions.

Furthermore, the AI Platform GCP provides an infrastructure for developing and deploying machine learning models, allowing DataOps teams to easily integrate artificial intelligence into their data pipelines.

Cost reduction and resource optimization

One of the great advantages of the cloud is the possibility of reducing costs through resource optimization. Instead of needing to invest in physical hardware, companies can use cloud services on demand, paying only for the resources they use. This translates into a more efficient and cost-effective model for implementing DataOps.

The use of solutions such as serverless computing and containers enables automatic scaling that optimizes resource usage. This is especially important for DataOps, where demand for processing and storage can vary depending on projects and data volume. With the use of containers, such as Kubernetes In the cloud, companies can create highly scalable development and production environments, ensuring data pipelines can run seamlessly and efficiently.

Another interesting approach is the use of multi-cloud architectures, where companies can distribute their data and processes between different cloud providers, ensuring greater resilience and cost optimization. For example, a company may choose to use the AWS for processing and the Azure for storage, taking advantage of the best of each platform according to your specific needs.

Furthermore, the tools resource monitoring in the cloud, like AWS CloudWatch, the Azure Monitor and the Google Stackdriver, offer detailed visibility into resource usage and can help companies identify optimization opportunities. These tools allow you to detect bottlenecks, adjust resource allocation and predict future scalability needs, contributing to more efficient management of operational costs.

Impact of the cloud on data agility

The integration of DataOps with the cloud results in a significant improvement in the agility of data processes. With cloud platforms, companies can quickly provision resources without the long wait times typical of traditional infrastructure. This speeds up the data lifecycle, allowing companies to make faster decisions based on more up-to-date data.

The cloud also facilitates collaboration between multidisciplinary teams. Cloud tools provide collaborative work environments and continuous integration (CI/CD) tools that enable development, operations, and data teams to work more efficiently and aligned, without the physical constraints of infrastructure.

Additionally, the flexibility of the cloud allows companies to experiment and implement new data models or processing solutions quickly and with lower financial risk. This ability to quickly test and adjust data solutions is critical in today's fast-paced world, where demands and markets are constantly changing.

Challenges and considerations

While the cloud offers a number of benefits for DataOps, there are some challenges that companies must consider. One of the biggest challenges is the **data security**. Although cloud platforms offer multiple layers of security, it is critical that companies implement additional measures to ensure the protection of sensitive data. The use of end-to-end encryption, strict access control, and data governance policies are essential to mitigate risk.

Another challenge is the cost management. Although the cloud offers a cost-effective solution, lack of adequate control over resource usage can result in high costs. Implementing good resource monitoring practices and using cost optimization tools are essential to avoid surprises on your cloud bill.

Finally, to legacy systems integration can be a hurdle for many companies moving to the cloud. While cloud platforms offer a wide range of integration tools, it may be necessary to adapt existing systems to work effectively with the new infrastructure. The transition to the cloud must be carefully planned to avoid disruptions to data flows and ensure that all systems work in harmony.

Cloud computing represents a significant change in the way data is managed and processed in companies. When combined with the agile DataOps approach, the cloud provides a scalable, flexible and optimized infrastructure for data management. Tools like AWS, Azure and GCP offer a range of solutions that enable the automation of data flows, building agile pipelines and real-time analysis. However, it is important for companies to be aware of the challenges related to security, cost management and integration with legacy systems when adopting cloud-based solutions for DataOps. With a well-defined strategy, companies can reap the benefits of this powerful combination, improving their data operations and gaining a significant competitive advantage.

CHAPTER 7 – DATA QUALITY AND GOVERNANCE

Data management in an organization goes far beyond simple storage or processing. It involves a series of practices and policies that ensure the integrity, security and compliance of data throughout its entire lifecycle. Data quality and governance have a direct impact on decision-making, regulatory compliance and the efficient operation of companies. In this chapter, we'll cover how to ensure data is always reliable, how to implement policies that promote effective governance, and how to detect and correct anomalies in data flows.

Ensuring data integrity, security and compliance

Data integrity refers to the accuracy and consistency of data throughout its entire lifecycle. Corrupt, incomplete or inaccurate data can generate wrong decisions, directly affecting business performance. To ensure integrity, the first action is to clearly define the data sources and processes that will be responsible for their collection, transformation and storage. Each data entry point must be validated for compliance with the organization's rules and criteria.

Data security, on the other hand, focuses on protecting data from unauthorized access, cyberattacks, or other forms of malicious manipulation. Implementing data security practices involves encryption, access control, continuous monitoring and data segmentation. This ensures that only authorized users can access or modify sensitive and critical data.

Compliance with regulations is a growing concern in organizations, especially with the implementation of legislation such as the GDPR (General Data Protection Regulation) in Europe and the LGPD (General Data Protection Law) in Brazil. To ensure compliance, companies must follow legal requirements related to the storage, use and sharing of personal data, offering transparency and control to the data subject.

Data governance tools, which include identity management, access control and monitoring solutions, play an important role in ensuring that all of these areas – integrity, security and compliance – are met effectively. The use of specific frameworks, such as COBIT (Control Objectives for Information and Related Technologies) ou o Data Management Body of Knowledge (DMBOK), provides guidelines on how to implement and monitor data governance in a structured and efficient way.

Methods for detecting and correcting anomalies

Anomaly detection and correction are essential components for maintaining data quality. Anomalies can occur for a variety of reasons: human errors during data entry, failures in automated systems, duplicate data or even integration problems between different data sources. These deviations can be harmful, impacting decision-making and, in extreme cases, resulting in compliance or security breaches.

To detect anomalies in data, it is necessary to apply real-time monitoring techniques, using monitoring tools. data observability. Observability refers to the ability to monitor, measure and analyze data flows and their quality over time. There are several tools on the market that can be configured to detect anomalies based on pre-established patterns.

Techniques for detecting anomalies:

1. **Data format and type validation**: Each dataset must have a specific format and type that meets the system requirements. Validation can be performed using regular expressions or type checking functions to ensure that the data received is in the correct format.
2. **Consistency check between interdependent data**: Data that refer to each other must be consistent. For example, if a date field contains a date of birth, an age field cannot have a contradictory value. Tools like **Great Expectations** offer libraries to create automatic validations that check data interdependencies.
3. **Statistical analysis of variability**: Statistical analysis can be used to identify variations in data. This may include checking for outliers, which are values that are too far away from the rest of the data. A popular tool for this is **Z-score**, which helps identify anomalies based on the mean and standard deviation of data.
4. **Trend analysis**: Data that follows patterns or trends can be monitored over time. The use of algorithms **machine learning** for time series analysis can identify when data deviates significantly from the expected trend, alerting you to possible problems.
5. **Real-time monitoring**: Use monitoring platforms such as **Apache Kafka**, **Prometheus** or **Grafana** can help detect failures in data flows in real time. These tools allow you to configure automated alerts, which inform you when specific data does not follow the established criteria.

Anomaly correction:

After detecting an anomaly, the next step is to correct it efficiently, which can be done through several approaches:

1. **Automated processing and cleaning**: The use of tools **ETL** (extraction, transformation and load) can be configured to automatically handle errors. These tools can perform erroneous value replacements, correct formatting or even delete duplicate data.
2. **Manual correction**: In cases where automation is not sufficient, manual intervention is necessary. To achieve this, a structured data review and approval process must be created. This process can be supported by data visualization tools, such as **Painting** or the **Power BI**, to quickly identify problems.
3. **Feedback to the source system**: When an anomaly is detected, it is essential that the system that originated the data is corrected to prevent the error from recurring. This feedback loop can be done through the implementation of **data gateways** and **log audit**, allowing the source of the error to be corrected in real time.
4. **Correction of historical data**: When the anomaly is not detected in time and affects historical data, it may be necessary to perform a retroactive correction. This involves reviewing large volumes of data and can be done through remediation scripts such as **SQL scripts** that adjust or delete erroneous records.

Implementation of Data Governance Policies

Data governance involves defining policies, processes and standards to ensure data is well managed and aligned with organizational objectives. Implementing these governance policies requires the creation of a robust framework that covers aspects such as access control, quality management, data security and legal compliance.

Establishing a governance framework

The first step to implementing data governance is defining a framework, which can be based on widely accepted standards, such as the DMBOK (Data Management Body of Knowledge) or the ISO/IEC 38500, which provides guidelines on effective IT management. This framework must be adapted to meet the specific needs of each organization and include processes to:

1. **Data classification and categorization**: Data must be classified according to its importance and sensitivity. For example, financial data may be classified as highly sensitive and require a higher level of protection.
2. **Definition of roles and responsibilities**: To ensure effective governance, it is necessary to assign clear roles and responsibilities to everyone involved in data management. These roles may include **Data Stewards** (responsible for data quality), **Data Owners** (responsible for data security and privacy) and **Data Custodians** (responsible for technical maintenance).
3. **Access and security policies**: Data governance must include clear rules and policies about who can access what data and under what conditions. This involves implementing **role-based access control (RBAC)** and defining encryption policies for data at rest and in transit.
4. **Compliance and audit policies**: Compliance with data protection regulations such as GDPR is essential. To ensure data is being managed legally and ethically, governance policies must include regular audits and compliance reviews.
5. **Documentation and transparency**: Data governance must be transparent and documented. This includes

recording all policies, processes, decisions and actions taken in relation to data. Documentation helps create a solid foundation for future training and audits.

Tools for data governance

There are several tools that can help organizations implement and maintain data governance practices. Some of the most used include:

1. **Cockroaches**: A data governance platform that offers solutions for data cataloguing, classification and compliance. It helps organizations manage their data more efficiently while maintaining quality and compliance.
2. **Informatica**: Offers a suite of tools for data governance, including solutions for **data lineage**, data integration and quality monitoring.
3. **Alation**: A data governance platform that focuses on creating a collaborative data catalog, enabling data teams to manage and share data more efficiently.

Data quality and governance are essential aspects to ensure that the data used in organizations is reliable, secure and compliant. Implementing governance practices, combined with anomaly detection and correction, provides the necessary foundation for using data effectively and ethically. Appropriate tools, such as those for data monitoring and management, play a crucial role at each step of this process, allowing companies to leverage their data with confidence and make decisions based on high-quality information. Additionally, a well-structured approach to data governance helps organizations remain compliant with regulations and protect sensitive information, promoting a culture of accountability and transparency in data management.

CHAPTER 8 – AUTOMATION AND CONTINUOUS INTEGRATION (CI/CD) FOR DATA

Automation and continuous integration (CI/CD) play a vital role in the DataOps process, being fundamental to improving efficiency, quality and agility in data management within organizations. In a world where data is increasingly dynamic and needs to be analyzed in real time, automating data flows and implementing continuous pipelines becomes not only desirable, but essential to ensure that companies remain competitive and can make the most of the value of data.

Using CI/CD in the context of DataOps means that the data lifecycle must be handled with the same efficiency and automation with which software development is handled. This includes building pipelines that allow data to be continuously integrated, tested and implemented in production systems, ensuring that any changes, updates or introduction of new data into the system happen quickly, without compromising the quality and integrity of the information.

The role of CI/CD in DataOps

CI/CD is a concept widely adopted in software development, but its application in the context of DataOps offers substantial benefits for data management. Automation, as part of a continuous integration strategy, is essential to ensure that the handling of data – from its collection to its use in analysis and reporting – is consistent and flawless.

Continuous Integration (CI) for Data

Continuous integration in the context of DataOps involves the process of frequently integrating new data or data changes into core systems in an automated manner. Instead of performing manual integrations that can be prone to errors or inconsistencies, CI promotes automation of the integration process, allowing data to flow seamlessly through pipelines. This includes:

- Data Collection: Automation starts with collecting data from various sources such as databases, APIs or files. Tools like Apache NiFi or StreamSets are widely used to orchestrate this data collection in real time, integrating heterogeneous data sources in a simplified and efficient way.

- Data Transformation: Once collected, data often needs to be transformed to fit the format and structure required by analysis or storage systems. Transformation tools such as Apache Spark or dbt, can be integrated into the pipeline to ensure that data is handled correctly and in an automated way.

- Data Storage: After transformation, data needs to be stored efficiently, on platforms that meet scalability and performance requirements. Continuous integration allows data to be stored automatically, whether in relational databases, data lakes or data warehouses.

Continuous Delivery (CD) for Data

While continuous integration focuses on ensuring that data is collected and transformed constantly and automatically, continuous delivery ensures that this transformed data is made available to analytics systems or end users continuously and without interruptions. Continuous delivery in the context of DataOps involves:

- **Automated Data Pipeline**: This pipeline includes automatic steps that collect, process, and store data continuously. This reduces the need for manual intervention, enabling rapid response to changes in data or analysis needs.

- **Data Monitoring and Validation**: After data delivery, it is important to monitor its quality and consistency. Continuous delivery not only makes data available, but also performs validations to ensure data complies with established governance policies. This is done using frameworks such as Great Expectations, which enables the automation of data testing to ensure that the data delivered is complete, accurate and valid.

Automated Testing and Data Validation

Validation and automated testing play a crucial role in maintaining data quality across the DataOps lifecycle. Automated testing ensures that the data being processed and delivered is of high quality and conforms to defined rules.

Data Validation in Continuous Integration

In continuous integration, the data validation process is performed whenever new data is integrated or modified into the system. This process verifies that data meets certain quality criteria, such as completeness, accuracy, and consistency. Validation can be done through simple rules, such as checking formats or detecting missing data, or through more complex validations, such as checking dependencies between different data sources.

Types of Automated Tests

Automated tests performed during the CI/CD cycle for data can include:

1. **Data Consistency Tests**: Checks whether data from different sources is consistent with each other. For example, it can be checked whether the "date of birth" field in one customer table matches the "age" field in another table.

2. **Referential Integrity Tests**: Ensure that relationships between different sets of data are valid. This is particularly important when working with data in relational systems, where integrity between tables must be maintained.

3. **Data Quality Tests**: Verifies that data meets defined criteria, such as not having null values in required fields, ensuring that values are within an expected range, or that data is in the correct format.

4. **Performance Tests**: Evaluate system response time when processing large volumes of data. Performance testing is essential to ensure that data pipelines do not fail when faced with high loads.

5. **Data security testing**: Validate whether data is being adequately protected during the collection, transformation and storage process. This includes checking encryption and controlling access to sensitive data.

Tools for Automated Data Testing

There are several tools that can be used to implement automated data testing within CI/CD pipelines:

1. **Great Expectations**: One of the most popular tools for data validation. It allows you to create tests and expectations to ensure that data meets defined quality and governance criteria. The platform can be integrated with tools such as **Apache Airflow** and **dbt** to orchestrate data testing in an automated way.
2. **Deequ**: A tool developed by Amazon, which allows you to perform data quality validations on large volumes. It integrates directly with **Apache Spark**, facilitating the execution of tests in distributed environments.
3. **Taurus**: For performance testing, Taurus offers a simplified interface for creating and running load tests, including data stored in systems such as **Kafka** or **Hadoop**.
4. **DataRobot**: Although it is largely associated with machine learning automation, DataRobot also offers capabilities to validate and ensure data integrity, especially when that data is used to train machine learning models.

Tools and Frameworks for Continuous Integration

Implementing CI/CD pipelines for data requires specialized tools and frameworks. These tools help to automate the integration, validation and data delivery steps, ensuring that all changes are processed in an efficient and controlled manner.

Pipeline Orchestration Tools

Orchestration tools are essential for managing the flow of data between the various stages of a CI/CD pipeline. These tools allow you to create, manage and monitor complex data pipelines, ensuring that all steps are executed in an orderly and efficient manner.

1. **Apache Airflow**: A workflow orchestration platform that makes it easy to schedule and execute data pipelines. Airflow allows you to configure complex data pipelines, with automated validation and transformation steps.
2. **Luigi**: Created by Spotify, Luigi is another workflow orchestration tool that can be used to manage and monitor data pipelines. Although it is less well-known than Airflow, it has a simple approach and is quite effective for managing large-scale data processing tasks.
3. **Kubeflow**: An open source platform designed to implement machine learning pipelines, but can also be adapted to manage data pipelines. The advantage of Kubeflow is its integration with Kubernetes, allowing pipelines to scale easily and efficiently.

Data Versioning Tools

Just like in software development, data versioning is essential to ensure that any changes made to data or pipelines are tracked and auditable. Data versioning tools help track modifications and make it easier to roll back unwanted changes.

1. **DVC (Data Version Control)**: DVC is a data versioning tool that integrates with Git, allowing data teams to control and version datasets, just like they do with source code.
2. **Delta Lake**: Delta Lake is a data storage layer that allows versioning of data within a **data lake**. It maintains a complete history of changes made to data and makes it easy to recover from previous versions.
3. **Git LFS**: Although Git LFS (Large File Storage) is not a data-only tool, it is very useful for versioning large datasets that are needed for training machine learning

models, for example.

Automation and continuous integration (CI/CD) in the context of DataOps are essential to ensure that data flows are efficient, secure, and of high quality. Implementing automated pipelines not only increases the agility of data processes, but also improves consistency and reliability, enabling companies to make decisions based on high-quality data. Orchestration tools, automated testing and data versioning are key components of this strategy, providing a continuous and controlled lifecycle for data. In an increasingly data-driven environment, adopting CI/CD practices has become a strategic necessity for organizations seeking to stand out in today's competitive market.

CHAPTER 9 – OBSERVABILITY AND DATA MONITORING

Data observability and monitoring play an essential role in maintaining the integrity, performance, and compliance of data systems. The ability to quickly track, audit and respond to incidents in the data stream not only improves reliability, but is also critical to ensuring that data is used effectively and within established standards. In a complex and dynamic data environment, where information can be generated and manipulated in large volume and speed, having adequate monitoring and observability tools and practices becomes essential.

Observability goes beyond simply collecting metrics, addressing the need to understand the behavior of a data system and the interactions between its components. This understanding is crucial for detecting anomalies, optimizing processes, and ensuring that data-driven decisions are informed by correct and reliable information.

How to track and audit data flows

Tracking and auditing data flows is an essential practice to ensure data quality, security, and compliance throughout its lifecycle. Traceability helps to identify the origin of the data, the processes it went through and the results obtained from its manipulation, ensuring transparency and allowing the audit of the system's behavior.

Data Traceability

Data traceability is a concept that refers to the complete monitoring of data from its origin to its final destination. This involves recording the transformations and movements that the data goes through, as well as documenting the sources and processes involved. Implementing efficient traceability in data pipelines requires a combination of tools, techniques and best practices.

One of the most common approaches to tracking data in streams is to use metadata, which describe and document important characteristics of the data, such as its format, origin, destination, those responsible for the transformation and the moments in which changes occurred. Metadata must be managed appropriately using data governance tools and must be accessible for query to enable tracking.

Tools like Apache Kafka and Apache NiFi are effective for real-time data collection and tracking. These tools enable the orchestration of data in motion and the creation of traceability logs that document each data event generated or manipulated. Using these platforms, it is possible to create pipelines that monitor data sources and track movements, ensuring that all changes can be audited efficiently.

Data Audit

Data auditing is critical to ensuring data is handled in a manner that complies with governance policies and compliance regulations. Auditing involves creating detailed records of all interactions with data, allowing any flaws or inconsistencies to be quickly identified.

An efficient data audit includes:

- **Access Log**: Monitor who accesses data and in what context to ensure that only authorized users can modify or query sensitive data.

- **Transformation Record**: Track all transformations that data has undergone throughout its life cycles. This registration can be done using tools such as **dbt** or **Apache Spark**, which allow you to document all stages of data processing and transformation.

- **Processing Logs**: Processing logs are vital for auditing, allowing you to verify that data was processed correctly and as expected. These logs can be analyzed to identify errors or failures in the data flow.

- **Regulatory Compliance**: An effective data audit also ensures that data handling complies with data protection regulations such as the **General Data Protection Law (LGPD)** or the **General Data Protection Regulation (GDPR)**.

Implementation of metrics and dashboards

The implementation of data monitoring metrics and dashboards is a practice that provides visibility into the performance of data systems and allows informed decision-making. Metrics help quantify essential aspects of data flow, such as response time, error rate, integrity, and availability, while dashboards provide a visual interface to track these metrics in real time.

Data Metrics

Data metrics are fundamental to understanding the state and performance of data systems and pipelines. Some essential metrics include:

- **Processing Latency**: Measures the time required to process a set of data, from its ingestion to its transformation and storage. Latency can be monitored using tools like Prometheus or Grafana, which allow you to track the execution time of processes and generate alerts when performance is below expectations.

- **Error Rate**: Error rate monitors how often failures occur in data processing. It can include validation errors, integration failures, or errors in transformation steps. Using tools like Datadog or Splunk, you can set up alerts to notify staff when error rates exceed pre-determined thresholds.
- **Data Quality**: Data quality must be measured continuously to ensure that the data delivered is accurate, complete, and consistent. This includes monitoring metrics such as the presence of null, duplicate, or inconsistent data. The tool Great Expectations can be used to measure and validate data quality in real time, automating verification of compliance with quality expectations.

- **Data Volume**: Measuring the volume of data being processed in real time helps you understand system behavior and identify bottlenecks or areas that may require optimization. Tools like Apache Kafka and Apache Flink can be used to monitor the volume of data in motion and adjust system resources as needed.

Monitoring Dashboards

Dashboards are essential for visualizing data metrics and providing quick insights into the state of data systems. Using visualization tools such as Grafana, Painting or Power BI, you can create personalized dashboards that show real-time performance and data health.

These dashboards should include key performance indicators (KPIs) that help data teams monitor system efficiency. Furthermore, dashboards must allow the visualization of metrics at different levels, so that the technical team can delve into more specific data, while business leaders have an overview of the metrics most relevant to the operation.

Dashboard Example for Data Monitoring

A basic example of a dashboard for data monitoring might include:

1. **Data Pipeline Status**: A line chart that shows the status of the data pipeline in real time, with visual indicators for latency and errors.
2. **Data Quality**: A bar chart that illustrates the percentage of valid, incomplete, and duplicate data. This can be supplemented with automatic alerts when data quality drops below an acceptable level.
3. **Volume of Data Processed**: An area chart that shows the volume of data processed in a specific time window, with indicators for traffic spikes or outlier volumes.
4. **Error Rate**: A bar chart that shows the failure rate in data pipelines, allowing the team to quickly identify failures at critical steps.

Incident analysis and failure response

Incident analysis and fault response are crucial activities to ensure that the data system remains available and functional. When failures or incidents occur, it is important that teams can quickly identify the root cause and take corrective action to minimize the impact.

Incident Analysis

Incident analysis begins with collecting detailed information about what occurred, when it occurred, and what the impact was. Monitoring tools like **Datadog**, **New Relic** and **Splunk** help generate logs and records that facilitate failure investigation.

Incident analysis should involve:

- **Log Review**: Examine the logs to identify any recurring patterns or errors that may have caused the failure. These logs must be detailed and stored centrally so that they can be easily accessed and analyzed during the investigation.

- **Root Cause Identification**: The root cause of an incident must be identified with the aim of preventing the failure from occurring again. This involves analyzing historical data, transformation processes, and interactions between systems to discover where data flow has been compromised.

Fault Response

After analyzing the incident, it is necessary to implement an effective response to mitigate the damage and correct the failure. The response must be agile and involve:

- **Immediate Fix**: Take quick corrective action, such as reprocessing data, correcting configurations, or temporarily stopping the pipeline to prevent error propagation.

- **Restore Compliance**: If the failure affected data compliance, you must restore compliance quickly to ensure your data is back in compliance with regulations and governance policies.

- **Preventing Future Incidents**: After fixing the flaw, the team must implement additional controls, such as automated tests and rechecks, to prevent similar flaws in the future.

Data observability and monitoring are essential elements for the health and efficiency of data systems. The ability to track and audit data streams, implement appropriate metrics and dashboards, and quickly respond to incidents allows organizations to maintain control over their operations and ensure data-driven decisions are reliable. Monitoring and observability tools and practices provide the means necessary to ensure data quality, security, and compliance, as well as help with early detection of issues and rapid response to failures.

CHAPTER 10 – DATAOPS FOR BUSINESS INTELLIGENCE (BI)

The application of Data Ops (data operations) in the area of Business Intelligence (BI) has been a growing trend in organizations seeking to optimize the manipulation, preparation and delivery of data for reports and dashboards. The combination of DataOps practices with BI offers substantial benefits, such as greater efficiency, reliability and agility in data transformation processes, directly contributing to faster and more informed business decisions. This chapter explores how DataOps can be used to improve reports and dashboards, as well as facilitate automation in data preparation and ingestion, highlighting the most common and effective tools in the BI context.

Using DataOps to improve reports and dashboards

Reports and dashboards are crucial tools for visualizing and analyzing data in organizations. However, the quality of these products directly depends on the way the data is prepared and manipulated. DataOps has the potential to transform the way data is processed, significantly improving the quality and reliability of information used in reports and dashboards. Implementing DataOps not only improves data accuracy, but also speeds up information delivery time and makes the reporting process more efficient.

The Integration of DataOps in the BI Process

Traditionally, BI processes involve extracting, transforming, and loading (ETL) large volumes of data from multiple sources into a central repository, such as a data warehouse. DataOps, when integrated into this process, can automate, monitor and improve ETL phases, ensuring that data is available for reports and dashboards with the greatest possible accuracy.

The use of automated data pipeline is an example of how DataOps can optimize the BI process. When using tools that automate the flow of data between systems, such as Apache Airflow or dbt, organizations can set up processes that ensure data is extracted and transformed consistently and without manual intervention. This reduces human error and improves the reliability of the data that feeds reports and dashboards.

Improving Data Quality

DataOps also improves data quality that feed the reports. Ensuring that data is consistent, complete and up-to-date is essential for reports and dashboards to provide reliable information. The use of DataOps practices, such as real-time data validation and the automated quality control, allows the BI team to quickly detect any issues with the data before it is used to make decisions.

Tools like Great Expectations can be integrated into the data pipeline to ensure that data meets specified quality criteria, such as the presence of null values, consistency between fields, and the absence of duplicates. These tools help automate error detection and ensure data is ready for analysis without the need for manual checks, which significantly speeds up report creation.

Accelerated Reporting Cycle Time

Another significant benefit of DataOps in creating reports and dashboards is the acceleration of the production cycle.

Automating data preparation steps such as cleaning and transformation allows data analysts to focus more on analyzing and interpreting data rather than spending time on repetitive, manual tasks. Furthermore, the continuous integration (CI) e a continuous delivery (CD) applied to the data lifecycle ensure that data updates are reflected in real time on dashboards, providing a more dynamic and accurate view for decision makers.

Better Collaboration between Data and Business Teams

One of the main advantages of integrating DataOps into the BI process is the improved collaboration between data teams and business areas. By establishing well-defined, automatic data pipelines, BI teams can quickly meet information demands from other areas of the company. DataOps facilitates communication between these teams by ensuring that data is always up to date and available, allowing business teams to efficiently obtain the insights they need.

By integrating DataOps practices with BI, it is also possible to configure interactive dashboards that enable business users to explore data in real time. For example, tools like Power BI or Painting can be configured to connect directly to data pipelines and show the most up-to-date information. This not only increases the effectiveness of reporting, but also gives decision makers the ability to explore the data on their own without relying on manual processes to obtain customized reports.

Automation in data preparation and ingestion

Automation in data preparation and ingestion is one of the fundamental pillars of DataOps. Data ingestion involves collecting information from multiple sources and processing it to ensure it is in the proper format for analysis. When done manually, this task is error-prone, time-consuming, and difficult to scale. Automating data ingestion using DataOps tools not only improves efficiency, but also allows organizations to process large volumes of data more quickly and with fewer resources.

Data Extraction Automation

A **data extraction** is the first step in the ETL process and involves collecting data from external sources such as databases, APIs, CSV files or business management systems. Using automated tools for this step allows data to be extracted efficiently and without manual intervention.

Tools like Apache NiFi or Talend can be configured to automatically extract data from different sources, using ready-made connectors for main data systems. These tools also offer the possibility to perform simple pre-processing, such as format conversions and data cleaning, before sending it to the next stage of the pipeline.

Automated Data Transformation

Data transformation is a critical step in the data preparation process as it involves changing the structure and enriching the data to make it more suitable for analysis. Traditionally, data transformations are performed by data analysts, but with the use of DataOps, these transformations can be automated.

Tools like dbt (data build tool) are widely used to define and automate data transformations. dbt allows analysts to write data transformations in SQL in a modular way, automatically applying them whenever new data is ingested. This significantly reduces time spent on manual tasks and ensures that transformations are consistent and reusable.

Data Load Automation

Data loading, which involves sending the transformed data to a central repository such as a data warehouse or analytics database, can also be automated. The use of tools such as Apache Airflow enables the creation of ingestion and load pipelines that run automatically, without the need for human intervention.

Furthermore, DataOps tools enable continuous integration (CI) e a continuous delivery (CD) in data context. This means that whenever a new transformation or improvement to the ingestion process is implemented, it can be automatically integrated into the pipeline and tested, ensuring that uploaded data is always compliant with company governance standards and policies.

Tools for BI and DataOps

There are several tools that can be used to integrate DataOps practices into the data lifecycle, improving the performance and effectiveness of the BI process. These tools are designed to automate, monitor and manage data flows, ensuring that reports and dashboards are based on reliable and up-to-date information.

Ingestion and ETL Tools

- **Apache Airflow**: It is one of the most popular tools for orchestrating workflows and data pipelines. It allows you to define and automate the steps of the ETL process, ensuring that data is extracted, transformed and loaded efficiently and reliably.

- **Talend**: A data integration platform that offers a wide range of connectors and tools for data ingestion and transformation. Talend enables workflow automation, real-time integrations and the performance of complex transformation tasks.

Data Preparation and Quality Tools

- **dbt**: It is a data transformation tool that allows data analysts to define transformations in a modular way using SQL, as well as automate the execution of these transformations whenever data is loaded into the system.

- **Great Expectations**: Tool data quality which allows you to automate checks to ensure that data meets specific quality criteria, such as the absence of null or duplicate values, before it is used in dashboards and reports.

BI and Data Visualization Tools

- **Power BI**: Widely used BI platform that allows you to integrate data from multiple sources and create interactive dashboards. Power BI can be connected directly to automated data pipelines, offering a real-time view of data.

- **Painting**: Another popular data visualization tool that can be integrated into automated data pipelines, allowing you to create dynamic, personalized dashboards that update in real time.

The integration of Data Ops in the practices of Business Intelligence (BI) offers an innovative and efficient approach to optimizing the preparation, transformation and delivery of data for reports and dashboards. By automating processes and improving data quality, DataOps helps organizations provide more accurate, faster and more reliable information to decision makers. Furthermore, the automation of data ingestion and transformation, as well as the use of specific tools for BI and DataOps, enable the creation of agile and scalable workflows, fundamental for building an efficient and effective BI system.

CAPÍTULO 11 – DATAOPS NO BIG DATA E MACHINE LEARNING

The integration of DataOps with Big Data and Machine Learning (ML) practices is becoming increasingly essential for organizations dealing with large volumes of data and looking to improve their predictive models. Operational efficiency and agility in data flows are key to ensuring that ML models are fed with high-quality data and that model lifecycles are optimized to ensure fast and accurate results. This chapter explores how DataOps can optimize Machine Learning models, automate the ML lifecycle, and which tools are most effective for combining DataOps with ML.

How DataOps optimizes Machine Learning models

Creating machine learning models depends on high-quality data and the ability to quickly iterate over different versions of the model. The practice of DataOps optimizes these steps, providing a continuous flow of data for training and evaluating models, as well as ensuring that the data pipeline is aligned with the needs of the model.

Ensuring Data Quality and Consistency

For an ML model to perform well, it needs to be fed high-quality data. DataOps helps ensure that the data used in an ML project is consistent, up-to-date, and error-free by implementing rigorous data management practices. data governance, real-time data validation and quality monitoring. This implies the use of tools that allow test and validate data as it is moved, ensuring that the datasets feeding the models are not corrupted along the way.

Tools like Great Expectations can be used to implement automated data validators that check data integrity, such as the absence of null values, consistency in columns and checking for duplicates. Automating these checks allows the data pipeline to continue flowing without the need for manual interventions, providing a continuous flow of data to ML models.

Data Pipeline Automation

The process of collecting and preparing data for ML training often involves performing repetitive and time-consuming tasks. With the implementation of DataOps, these tasks can be automated, ensuring that data is ready to feed models in a shorter time and with greater accuracy.

An example of this is the automation of data transformation with tools such as dbt (data build tool), which allows you to write SQL transformations that are automatically applied to data sets as they are loaded into the system. These transformations include data cleaning, aggregations, normalization, and other changes necessary to make the data more suitable for model training.

Real-Time Data Monitoring and Control

Another significant benefit of DataOps in ML is continuous monitoring of the data pipeline. This is crucial because in Big Data and ML environments, data can constantly change and sources can be dynamic, requiring adjustments to the model to reflect these changes. DataOps makes it easy to real-time monitoring of the data pipeline, enabling data teams to quickly identify and fix issues.

Using tools like Apache Kafka for data streaming and Apache Airflow for workflow orchestration, it is possible to ensure that the data that feeds ML models is always up to date and in the appropriate format. This provides immediate feedback, allowing ML models to be fine-tuned based on new data inputs.

ML lifecycle automation with DataOps

The Machine Learning lifecycle involves several steps, from data collection to deploying the model into production. DataOps can automate and manage these steps more efficiently, which allows ML models to be trained, tested, validated, and deployed continuously without the need for manual or time-consuming processes.

Automation in Data Collection and Preparation

The first step in the lifecycle of an ML model is the data collection. Data from multiple sources needs to be brought together, cleaned, and transformed to ensure it is ready for analysis. With the use of DataOps, it is possible automate this data ingestion through continuous data pipelines.

For example, using Apache NiFi, you can configure data flows to collect data from different sources and transform it as needed before passing it to your ML model. This allows data collection to be done automatically and in real time, without the need for human intervention.

Automation in Model Training

ML model training involves creating and running machine learning algorithms on data to generate a model that makes predictions or classifications. Automating this step is essential, as it allows the training process to be carried out continuously and in real time.

Using automation tools like Kubeflow, you can orchestrate the entire model lifecycle, from training to deployment. Kubeflow allows you to create pipelines de Machine Learning which run automatically each time new data is available, ensuring the model is continually trained with the latest data.

Example code for training automation with Kubeflow:

python

```python
import kfp
from kfp import dsl

@dsl.pipeline(
    name='ML Pipeline',
    description='An example ML pipeline'
)
def ml_pipeline():
    # Step 1: Data Preprocessing
    preprocess_op = dsl.ContainerOp(
        name='Preprocess Data',
        image='your_preprocessing_image',
        arguments=['--input', 'raw_data', '--output', 'clean_data']
    )

    # Step 2: Train Model
    train_op = dsl.ContainerOp(
        name='Train Model',
        image='your_training_image',
        arguments=['--data', 'clean_data', '--model', 'model_output']
    ).after(preprocess_op)

    # Step 3: Evaluate Model
    evaluate_op = dsl.ContainerOp(
        name='Evaluate Model',
        image='your_evaluation_image',
        arguments=['--model', 'model_output']
    ).after(train_op)
```

```
# Compile and run pipeline
kfp.Client().create_run_from_pipeline_func(ml_pipeline,
arguments={})
```

This pipeline automates the model preprocessing, training, and evaluation steps, ensuring that the model lifecycle is repeated continuously and without manual intervention.

Deployment and Monitoring of Models in Production

Once the model is trained and evaluated, it needs to be deployed to production. The automation of the continuous deployment of templates is crucial to ensure that the latest template is used by production applications.

Tools like MLflow and TensorFlow Extended (TFX) can be used to automate the process of model deployment, continuously monitoring models in production and offering mechanisms for managing model versions.

Code example to deploy and monitor a model with MLflow:

python

```
import mlflow
import mlflow.sklearn
from sklearn.model_selection import train_test_split
from sklearn.ensemble import RandomForestClassifier

# Load and split data
X, y = load_data()
X_train, X_test, y_train, y_test = train_test_split(X, y,
test_size=0.2)

# Model training
model = RandomForestClassifier(n_estimators=100)
model.fit(X_train, y_train)
```

```
# Model log in MLflow
with mlflow.start_run():
    mlflow.sklearn.log_model(model, "model")
    mlflow.log_params({"n_estimators": 100})

# Monitor the model in production
mlflow.pyfunc.load_model("model")
```

This example shows how to train a model, log it into MLflow, and deploy it in an automated way, allowing developers and data engineers to efficiently manage and monitor production model versions.

Tools for ML and DataOps combined

There are several tools that can be used to combine Data Ops with Machine Learning and Big Data. These tools ensure data is ready for ML models, automate model training and deployment, and enable continuous monitoring of model performance in production.

Data and ML Pipeline Automation Tools

- **Kubeflow**: A platform for orchestrating ML pipelines in **Kubernetes**, enabling automation of the complete ML lifecycle, from data preprocessing to model deployment and monitoring.

- **MLflow**: An open source platform for managing the lifecycle of ML models, including experiments, reproducibility, and deployment.

- **TensorFlow Extended (TFX)**: A set of tools for orchestrating ML pipelines, with a focus on **continuous integration** and **continuous delivery** of models in production.

Data Monitoring and Governance Tools

- **Apache Kafka**: A distributed streaming platform that can be used to manage real-time data streams and ensure the latest data is fed into ML models.

- **Great Expectations**: A tool that offers automated data testing and real-time data validation, ensuring the quality of the data that feeds ML models.

The combination of Data Ops with Machine Learning and Big Data enables organizations to handle large volumes of data efficiently, automate the lifecycle of their models, and improve the quality and reliability of the data used in their predictive models. With the use of specific tools and platforms, such as Kubeflow, MLflow and TensorFlow Extended, it is possible to automate the model ingestion, transformation, training and deployment steps, ensuring that data operations are aligned with Machine Learning and Big Data objectives. By adopting DataOps practices, organizations can reduce the time required to train and deploy models, improve data quality, and ensure that models in production are continually monitored and tuned.

CHAPTER 12 – DATAOPS IN FINANCE AND BANKING

The implementation of DataOps in the financial and banking sector is transforming the way institutions deal with large volumes of data, ensuring compliance, increasing transaction security and reducing fraud through pipeline automation. Adopting DataOps strategies allows banks and financial companies to improve operational efficiency, optimize fraud detection, and ensure compliance with stringent regulations. Applying these practices not only reduces risks, but also improves the customer experience and strengthens the institutions' reputation in the market.

Compliance and security in financial transactions

Regulation in the financial sector is one of the most critical aspects for any banking institution. Regulatory bodies require banks and companies in the sector to maintain detailed records of transactions, ensuring transparency and preventing illicit activities, such as money laundering and terrorist financing. Implementing DataOps significantly improves the ability to meet these requirements by structuring automated and traceable processes for collecting, validating and storing financial data.

Continuous monitoring and auditing

Automation of monitoring processes ensures that all transactions are recorded and analyzed in real time. DataOps tools such as Apache Kafka and Considerable, enable the capture and continuous processing of data streams, ensuring that any anomaly is detected instantly.

Example code for capturing financial events with Kafka:

python

```
from kafka import KafkaConsumer

consumer = KafkaConsumer(
    'financial_transactions',
    bootstrap_servers='localhost:9092',
    auto_offset_reset='earliest',
    enable_auto_commit=True,
    value_deserializer=lambda x: x.decode('utf-8')
)

for message in consumer:
    transaction = message.value
    print(f"Transaction received: {transaction}")
```

This script captures financial transactions in real time, ensuring that all events are processed and analyzed continuously.

Validation and data quality

Financial transactions need to be validated to prevent errors, fraud and compliance violations. The application of DataOps in this context involves the use of tools that guarantee the data quality before they are processed or stored. Tools like Great Expectations allow you to automatically validate the structure and consistency of data.

Code for validating financial data:

python

```
from great_expectations.dataset import PandasDataset
import pandas as pd
```

```
data = pd.DataFrame({
    "transaction_id": [101, 102, 103],
    "amount": [500, -100, 700],
    "currency": ["USD", "USD", "EUR"]
})

dataset = PandasDataset(data)

assert dataset.expect_column_values_to_be_between("amount",
0, 10000).success
assert dataset.expect_column_values_to_be_in_set("currency",
["USD", "EUR", "GBP"]).success
```

This code ensures that negative values or invalid currencies are automatically detected and corrected before they are processed.

Reducing fraud with automated pipelines

Fraud detection in the financial sector requires analyzing patterns and recognizing suspicious behavior in real time. Machine Learning models combined with DataOps significantly increase accuracy in fraud detection, ensuring that fraudulent transactions are identified before they are completed.

Implementation of fraud detection pipelines

Creating an automated fraud analysis pipeline involves multiple steps, including data collection, pre-processing, and application of predictive algorithms. The use of tools such as Apache Airflow allows these steps to be organized and executed in a continuous and automated manner.

Code for a fraud detection pipeline with Airflow:

python

```
from airflow import DAG
```

```python
from airflow.operators.python import PythonOperator
from datetime import datetime
import pandas as pd

def fetch_transactions():
    data = pd.read_csv('/data/transactions.csv')
    return data

def detect_fraud():
    data = fetch_transactions()
    fraud_cases = data[data['amount'] > 10000]
    fraud_cases.to_csv('/data/suspect_transactions.csv',
index=False)

with DAG('fraud_detection_pipeline', start_date=datetime(2024,
1, 1), schedule_interval='@daily') as dag:
    fetch_data = PythonOperator(task_id='fetch_data',
python_callable=fetch_transactions)
    analyze_fraud = PythonOperator(task_id='analyze_fraud',
python_callable=detect_fraud)

    fetch_data >> analyze_fraud
```

This pipeline collects transactions daily, identifies suspicious movements and stores the cases for later analysis.

Machine Learning Models for Anomaly Detection

Using machine learning models for fraud detection allows fraudulent patterns to be recognized automatically. Algorithms like Isolation Forest are effective for identifying anomalies in large volumes of financial data.

Code to detect suspicious transactions using Isolation Forest:

python

```python
from sklearn.ensemble import IsolationForest
```

```
import pandas as pd

data = pd.read_csv('/data/transactions.csv')

model = IsolationForest(n_estimators=100, contamination=0.01)
data['fraud_score'] = model.fit_predict(data[['amount',
'transaction_time']])

suspicious_transactions = data[data['fraud_score'] == -1]
suspicious_transactions.to_csv('/data/fraud_cases.csv',
index=False)
```

This code trains a model to identify suspicious transactions and saves detected cases for analysis.

Case studies of banks that adopted DataOps

Case 1: Compliance automation in a multinational bank

A large multinational bank was struggling to ensure compliance with international regulations due to the high volume of daily transactions. The implementation of DataOps solved this problem by introducing automated pipelines for collecting, analyzing and archiving financial records, ensuring that all transactions were traceable and auditable.

The adoption of Apache NiFi for data ingestion, combined with Elastic Stack for monitoring, it allowed the bank to reduce regulatory audit time from weeks to hours, increasing transparency and reducing the risk of fines.

Case 2: Reducing fraud in a fintech

A fintech specialized in digital payments suffered from a high rate of fraud due to attempted fraudulent transactions in real time. With the implementation of DataOps, a continuous analysis pipeline was created using Apache Flink to process events in real time and a Machine Learning model to detect suspicious patterns.

As a result, the company reduced fraud by 30% in the first six months and improved user experience by reducing false positives in legitimate transactions.

Case 3: Optimizing the customer experience in a digital bank

A digital bank sought to improve its response to customer requests by automating credit analysis and transaction approval processes. With DataOps, the company implemented a continuous data pipeline using Apache Airflow and BigQuery, allowing you to process millions of transactions in seconds.

Automation ensured that customers received faster responses to credit requests, increasing satisfaction and optimizing service efficiency.

The implementation of DataOps in the financial sector provides significant strategic advantages, from ensuring security and compliance until improving the fraud detection and improve the operational efficiency. Pipeline automation reduces manual errors, speeds up response to suspicious transactions, and strengthens data governance. The use of tools such as Kafka, Airflow, MLflow and Apache Flink enables banks and fintechs to create scalable and reliable data streams, ensuring data quality and regulatory compliance.

The continuous advancement of DataOps practices will allow the financial sector to become even more agile and secure, enabling the creation of more efficient services that are protected against threats.

CHAPTER 13 – DATAOPS IN E-COMMERCE AND MARKETING

The adoption of DataOps in e-commerce and digital marketing is revolutionizing the way companies analyze and use data to personalize campaigns, automate segmentations and optimize the customer experience. The integration of dynamic data pipelines allows decision-making based on information updated in real time, ensuring greater precision in identifying consumption patterns, preferences and user behavior.

Personalizing campaigns with real-time data

The personalization of marketing campaigns is a determining factor in the success of companies in digital retail. Using DataOps allows marketing teams to analyze data instantly, adjusting promotions and communications based on customer behavior.

Continuous data collection and processing

The first step to effective personalization is capturing browsing, interaction and purchasing data. The use of Apache Kafka and Considerable Enables real-time processing of user-generated events, ensuring insights are extracted without delay.

Code for capturing navigation events with Kafka:

python

```
from kafka import KafkaProducer
```

```
import json

producer = KafkaProducer(
    bootstrap_servers='localhost:9092',
    value_serializer=lambda v: json.dumps(v).encode('utf-8')
)

event = {
    "user_id": 12345,
    "page": "/product/5678",
    "action": "view",
    "timestamp": "2025-02-10T12:30:45"
}

producer.send('user_interactions', value=event)
```

This code captures user navigation events and sends them to a Kafka topic, enabling immediate processing by analytics systems.

Real-time recommendation algorithms

Using recommendation algorithms improves user experience by suggesting personalized products based on browsing history. Models based on k-Nearest Neighbors (k-NN) or neural networks can be implemented to generate automatic suggestions.

Code for product recommendation with scikit-learn:

python

```
from sklearn.neighbors import NearestNeighbors
import numpy as np

# Simulation of customer preference vectors
user_preferences = np.array([
    [0.8, 0.2, 0.4],
    [0.3, 0.9, 0.7],
    [0.5, 0.6, 0.1]
```

```
])

model = NearestNeighbors(n_neighbors=2, metric='euclidean')
model.fit(user_preferences)

# Simulation of a new user
new_user = np.array([[0.7, 0.3, 0.4]])
_, indices = model.kneighbors(new_user)

print(f"Recommended products for the user: {indices}")
```

This code identifies products closest to a new user's profile, allowing for more accurate recommendations.

Automation in customer segmentation

Customer segmentation plays a crucial role in digital marketing, allowing campaigns to be targeted at specific audiences. Implementing automated pipelines with DataOps improves the efficiency of this process, ensuring that segments are constantly updated.

Automated customer classification

The use of segmentation clusters allows you to group customers with similar characteristics, optimizing campaign targeting. Algorithms like K-Means are widely used for this purpose.

Code for customer segmentation with K-Means:

python

```
from sklearn.cluster import KMeans
import pandas as pd

# Customer data simulation
```

```python
data = pd.DataFrame({
    "customer_id": [1, 2, 3, 4, 5],
    "spending_score": [60, 20, 80, 30, 90],
    "purchase_frequency": [10, 2, 15, 5, 18]
})

model = KMeans(n_clusters=2)
data['segment'] = model.fit_predict(data[['spending_score',
'purchase_frequency']])

print(data)
```

This code groups customers based on purchase volume and transaction frequency, allowing for more strategic segmentation.

Campaign automation with Airflow

The use of Apache Airflow enables the automation of campaign sending according to customer behavior.

Code for an automated marketing pipeline:

python

```python
from airflow import DAG
from airflow.operators.python import PythonOperator
from datetime import datetime

def fetch_new_customers():
    print("Fetching new customers from database...")

def send_promotions():
    print("Sending targeted promotions...")

with DAG('marketing_automation', start_date=datetime(2024, 1,
1), schedule_interval='@daily') as dag:
    task_fetch = PythonOperator(task_id='fetch_customers',
python_callable=fetch_new_customers)
```

```
task_send = PythonOperator(task_id='send_promotions',
python_callable=send_promotions)

task_fetch >> task_send
```

This code ensures that customers are automatically segmented and receive personalized campaigns.

Examples of success in digital retail

Case 1: Increased conversion with personalization in an online store

A large e-commerce platform implemented DataOps to process user data in real time. Analysis of browsing and purchasing behavior allowed personalized offers to be presented to each customer, increasing the conversion rate by 35%.

The use of Apache Spark Streaming enabled large-scale event capture and analysis, ensuring recommendations were made without delay.

Case 2: Smart segmentation in a fashion company

A digital fashion company used Machine Learning to create dynamic customer segments. Implementing predictive models has resulted in more effective campaigns, reducing customer acquisition costs and increasing engagement with targeted promotions.

The integration of BigQuery e Google Cloud Functions allowed the rapid processing of large volumes of data, optimizing campaign response time.

Case 3: Churn reduction in a marketplace

A marketplace detected that many customers abandoned their

cart before completing their purchase. With the implementation of DataOps, automated alerts were created to re-engage these users through personalized emails and notifications.

Cart recovery rate increased by 20%, demonstrating the effectiveness of data-driven automation.

The implementation of DataOps in e-commerce and digital marketing provides competitive advantages by allowing real-time personalization, automation in customer segmentation and continuous campaign optimization. The integration of technologies such as Kafka, Airflow, Spark e Machine Learning ensures that data is analyzed and used efficiently, resulting in greater customer conversion and retention.

Digital transformation in retail is increasingly dependent on data-driven strategies. The advancement of DataOps will allow companies to continue innovating, ensuring personalized and optimized experiences for consumers.

CHAPTER 14 – DATAOPS FOR HEALTHCARE AND BIOTECHNOLOGY

The application of DataOps in healthcare and biotechnology is transforming the way medical and genomic data is processed, stored and used. Optimizing data flows enables faster diagnoses, advanced biomedical research, and greater precision in personalized medicine. The adoption of automated pipelines and artificial intelligence solutions contributes to reducing errors, improving the efficiency of hospital systems and facilitating compliance with strict regulations.

Optimization of medical and genomic data

The collection and processing of medical data are fundamental challenges in the digitalization of healthcare. Hospital systems generate large volumes of information, from electronic patient records to high-resolution medical images. The application of DataOps allows automation in the ingestion, cleaning and organization of this data, ensuring availability for analysis in real time.

Healthcare data integration

Hospitals and clinics use several systems to store information, such as Electronic Patient Records (PEP) and Diagnostic Images (DICOM). The unification of this data allows for more efficient service and reduces redundancies.

Code for automated medical data ingestion with Apache NiFi:

python

```python
from nifiapi import NiFiClient

client = NiFiClient(url='http://localhost:8080/nifi-api')

dataflow = {
    "source": "hospital_database",
    "destination": "data_lake",
    "transformation": {
        "remove_nulls": True,
        "standardize_dates": True
    }
}

client.deploy_dataflow(dataflow)
```

This code automates the extraction of data from a hospital database to a Data Lake, eliminating inconsistencies before storage.

Genomic data processing

Genomic analysis generates massive volumes of information, requiring efficient pipelines for processing. Technologies like **Nextflow** enable the automation of large-scale analyses.

Code for genomic analysis pipeline:

nextflow

```nextflow
process ALIGN_READS {
    input:
    path reads from reads_dir
```

```
output:
path "aligned.bam"

script:
"""
bwa mem reference.fasta $reads > aligned.bam
"""
}
```

This pipeline aligns genetic sequences against a reference genome, allowing the identification of mutations relevant for diagnosis.

Challenges and regulations in digital health

The application of DataOps in healthcare requires compliance with strict regulations, ensuring the privacy and security of patient data.

Compliance with international standards

Several regulatory standards need to be followed when handling medical data, such as:

- **HIPAA (Health Insurance Portability and Accountability Act)** in the USA.

- **GDPR (General Data Protection Regulation)** in the European Union.

- **LGPD (General Data Protection Law)** in Brazil.

The implementation of anonymization mechanisms is essential to protect sensitive information.

STUDIOD21 SMART TECH CONTENT

Code for anonymizing medical records with Pandas:

python

```
import pandas as pd
from faker import Faker

fake = Faker()
df = pd.read_csv("patient_data.csv")

df["name"] = df["name"].apply(lambda x: fake.name())
df["birthdate"] = df["birthdate"].apply(lambda x:
fake.date_of_birth())

df.to_csv("anonymized_data.csv", index=False)
```

This code replaces real names and dates with fictitious values, ensuring privacy when sharing data for research.

Security and access control

Implementing strengthened authentication prevents unauthorized access to medical data. The use of OAuth 2.0 and role-based permissions control (RBAC) improves security.

Authentication with Flask and OAuth:

python

```
from flask import Flask, redirect, request, session
from authlib.integrations.flask_client import OAuth

app = Flask(__name__)
app.secret_key = "secure_key"
oauth = OAuth(app)

auth0 = oauth.register(
    'auth0',
```

```
    client_id='YOUR_CLIENT_ID',
    client_secret='YOUR_CLIENT_SECRET',
    authorize_url='https://yourdomain.auth0.com/authorize',
    access_token_url='https://yourdomain.auth0.com/oauth/
token'
)

@app.route('/login')
def login():
    return auth0.authorize_redirect(redirect_uri='http://
localhost:5000/callback')

@app.route('/callback')
def callback():
    auth0.authorize_access_token()
    return "User authenticated!"

if __name__ == '__main__':
    app.run(debug=True)
```

This code implements secure authentication to protect access to medical data.

Applications in biomedical research and AI

The combination of DataOps with artificial intelligence has accelerated advances in biomedical research, allowing everything from the discovery of new medicines to the development of predictive models for diagnoses.

Disease Detection with Machine Learning

Models of Machine Learning they can identify patterns in medical images, helping to diagnose diseases such as cancer.

Code for medical image classification with TensorFlow:

python

```
import tensorflow as tf
from tensorflow.keras import layers, models

model = models.Sequential([
    layers.Conv2D(32, (3,3), activation='relu', input_shape=(128, 128, 3)),
    layers.MaxPooling2D(2,2),
    layers.Conv2D(64, (3,3), activation='relu'),
    layers.MaxPooling2D(2,2),
    layers.Flatten(),
    layers.Dense(128, activation='relu'),
    layers.Dense(1, activation='sigmoid')
])

model.compile(optimizer='adam', loss='binary_crossentropy', metrics=['accuracy'])
```

This model is used to classify medical images and assist doctors in making accurate diagnoses.

Clinical trial automation

Optimizing data collection and analysis in clinical trials reduces costs and accelerates the discovery of new treatments.

Automated clinical trial monitoring with Python:

python

```
import requests
import json

def fetch_clinical_trials():
    url = "https://clinicaltrials.gov/api/query/study_fields?
expr=cancer&fields=NCTId,Condition,Status&format=json"
    response = requests.get(url)
```

```
data = response.json()
return data["StudyFieldsResponse"]["StudyFields"]

clinical_trials = fetch_clinical_trials()
print(clinical_trials)
```

This code queries data from ongoing clinical trials, facilitating the analysis of new medical research.

The adoption of DataOps in healthcare and biotechnology allows the optimization of medical and genomic data flows, ensuring greater efficiency in diagnoses and research. Automation in information collection, processing and analysis reduces failures and improves data security, ensuring compliance with global regulations.

The use of artificial intelligence in conjunction with data pipelines enables significant advances in biomedical research, enabling faster and more accurate discoveries. The future of digital medicine depends on the evolution of these technologies, ensuring personalized treatments and greater accessibility to healthcare.

CHAPTER 15 – STRATEGIES FOR DATAOPS TEAMS

The effective implementation of DataOps directly depends on the composition of well-structured teams and the use of appropriate tools for collaboration and productivity. An efficient team must have experts who can handle pipeline automation, data governance, and workflow optimization. Alignment between the roles of engineers, analysts, and DevOps professionals is critical to ensuring the continuous delivery of quality data for analytics and machine learning.

How to build an efficient DataOps team

Structuring a DataOps team involves combining technical and operational skills. The integration between different areas allows the creation of efficient and resilient pipelines, guaranteeing the reliability of the processed data.

Definition of responsibilities

Each team member needs to have well-defined roles to avoid task overlap and improve workflow efficiency. A well-structured team includes:

- **Data Engineers**: responsible for the construction and maintenance of pipelines.

- **Data Analysts**: focused on the interpretation and strategic use of data.

- **DevOps experts**: responsible for automation, monitoring and scalability of the infrastructure.

- **Gerente de DataOps**: coordinates the team and ensures adherence to good practices.

Automation culture

The DataOps philosophy prioritizes automation to eliminate bottlenecks in data processing. The team must adopt practices such as Infrastructure as Code (IaC) and Continuous Integration/ Continuous Deployment (CI/CD) to accelerate the delivery of quality data.

Code for automatic infrastructure provisioning with Terraform:

hcl

```
provider "aws" {
  region = "us-east-1"
}

resource "aws_s3_bucket" "data_lake" {
  bucket = "dataops-bucket"
  acl    = "private"
}

resource "aws_glue_catalog_database" "database" {
  name = "dataops_db"
}
```

This code creates a Data Lake on AWS automatically, enabling scalability without manual intervention.

Essential roles: engineers, analysts and DevOps

Collaboration between different specialists on the DataOps team is essential for process efficiency. Each one has specific duties that directly impact the quality and speed of data processing.

Data Engineer

The data engineer is responsible for building pipelines that extract, transform and load (ETL) information. It implements mechanisms to ensure the integrity and scalability of the data flow.

Code for ETL pipeline using Apache Airflow:

python

```
from airflow import DAG
from airflow.operators.python_operator import PythonOperator
from datetime import datetime
import pandas as pd

def extract():
    data = pd.read_csv("source_data.csv")
    return data

def transform(**context):
    data = context['task_instance'].xcom_pull(task_ids='extract')
    data["processed_date"] = datetime.now()
    return data

def load(**context):
    data =
context['task_instance'].xcom_pull(task_ids='transform')
    data.to_csv("processed_data.csv", index=False)

day = DAY('dataops_etl', schedule_interval="@daily",
start_date=datetime(2024, 1, 1))
```

```
task1 = PythonOperator(task_id='extract',
python_callable=extract, dag=dag)
task2 = PythonOperator(task_id='transform',
python_callable=transform, provide_context=True, dag=dag)
task3 = PythonOperator(task_id='load', python_callable=load,
provide_context=True, dag=dag)

task1 >> task2 >> task3
```

This code defines an ETL pipeline in **Apache Airflow**, allowing the automation of data processing.

Data Analyst

The data analyst focuses on extracting strategic insights. It uses visualization and modeling techniques to interpret patterns and trends.

Code for exploratory analysis with Python and Pandas:

python

```
import pandas as pd
import matplotlib.pyplot as plt

df = pd.read_csv("processed_data.csv")

df["category"].value_counts().plot(kind="bar", title="Category
Distribution")
plt.show()
```

This code generates a category distribution graph from the processed data, facilitating the identification of patterns.

DevOps Specialist

The DevOps specialist ensures that DataOps applications and pipelines are scalable, secure and monitored. It uses tools for deployment automation and continuous monitoring.

Code for CI/CD automation with GitHub Actions:

yaml

```
name: CI/CD Pipeline

on:
  push:
    branches:
      - main

jobs:
  deploy:
    runs-on: ubuntu-latest
    steps:
      - name: Checkout repository
        uses: actions/checkout@v3

      - name: Set up Python
        uses: actions/setup-python@v3
        with:
          python-version: '3.8'

      - name: Install dependencies
        run: pip install -r requirements.txt

      - name: Run tests
        run: pytest
```

This code configures a pipelinedeCI/CD which automatically runs tests when pushing code to the repository.

Tools for collaboration and productivity

Collaboration between DataOps team members depends on tools that facilitate communication, version control and pipeline monitoring.

Version control with Git and DVC

The use of Git combined with Data Version Control (DVC) allows you to manage code versions and datasets simultaneously.

Code for tracking large files with DVC:

bash

```
git init
dvc init
dvc add large_dataset.csv
git add large_dataset.csv.dvc .gitignore
git commit -m "Add dataset tracking with DVC"
```

This flow ensures that large volume files are versioned without overloading the Git repository.

Monitoring with Prometheus and Grafana

Pipeline observability is essential to quickly detect failures. Prometheus collects metrics while Grafana visualize the data.

Code for configuring monitoring with Prometheus:

yaml

```
global:
  scrape_interval: 15s

scrape_configs:
  - job_name: 'dataops_pipeline'
```

```
static_configs:
  - targets: ['localhost:8000']
```

This file configures a scraper do Prometheus, collecting metrics from DataOps pipelines.

The efficiency of a DataOps team depends on the organization of roles and the use of tools that promote automation, collaboration and continuous monitoring. Engineers, analysts and DevOps specialists must work in an integrated manner to ensure reliable and scalable pipelines. The adoption of practices such as CI/CD, Data Versioning and proactive monitoring strengthens the robustness of operations, allowing greater quality and speed in data delivery.

CHAPTER 16 – SECURITY AND PRIVACY IN DATAOPS

Security and privacy are fundamental aspects of DataOps, especially due to increased regulations on data protection and the growth of cyber threats. Implementing effective strategies for sensitive data protection and regulatory compliance ensures that data flows are protected from unauthorized access and leaks. The use of specific security frameworks strengthens the infrastructure and prevents compromises that could impact critical operations.

Sensitive data protection and regulatory compliance

Data security in DataOps starts with identifying and categorizing sensitive information. Financial, medical, personal and strategic data require strict controls to prevent unauthorized access. The implementation of encryption, anonymization and access control mechanisms is essential to guarantee the protection of this information.

Data Classification

Data categorization allows you to define specific policies for each type of information stored and processed. Data can be classified as:

- **Public Data**: information accessible without restrictions.

- **Internal Data**: used within the organization, but without sensitive information.

- **Sensitive Data**: Personal, financial or medical information that requires additional protection.

- **Critical Data**: data whose exposure could compromise operations or cause severe financial and reputational impacts.

Example automated data classification with Python:

python

```python
import pandas as pd

def classify_data(df):
    classification = {}
    for column in df.columns:
        if "credit_card" in column or "ssn" in column:
            classification[column] = "Sensitive"
        elif "email" in column or "phone" in column:
            classification[column] = "Internal"
        else:
            classification[column] = "Public"
    return classification

data = pd.read_csv("customer_data.csv")
print(classify_data(data))
```

This code identifies columns with sensitive information and automatically classifies them, allowing security policies to be applied.

Encryption and anonymization

Encryption protects data at rest and in transit, making unauthorized reading virtually impossible without the correct key. Anonymization removes or transforms sensitive information, ensuring that data can be used without compromising individuals' privacy.

Code model for data encryption with Python and the library Fernet do Cryptography:

python

```
from cryptography.fernet import Fernet

key = Fernet.generate_key()
cipher = Fernet(key)

sensitive_data = "1234-5678-9012-3456"
encrypted_data = cipher.encrypt(sensitive_data.encode())

print("Encrypted:", encrypted_data)
print("Decrypted:", cipher.decrypt(encrypted_data).decode())
```

This code generates an encryption key and protects a credit card number. Decryption can only be done with the correct key.

Compliance with regulations

Various regulations determine how data must be protected and processed. Some of the key legislation includes:

- **GDPR (General Data Protection Regulation – Europe):** Requires explicit consent for the collection and use of personal data.

- **LGPD (General Data Protection Law – Brazil)**: establishes guidelines similar to the GDPR, applied to Brazilian territory.

- **HIPAA (Health Insurance Portability and Accountability Act – EUA)**: regulates the protection of medical data.

Companies operating in multiple countries need to adapt their data flows to comply with all applicable legislation.

How to deal with leaks and cyber attacks

Detecting and mitigating cyber threats is critical to preventing data compromises. Leaks can occur due to human error, external attacks or infrastructure vulnerabilities.

Anomaly detection

Continuous monitoring of data streams can identify suspicious activity before a breach occurs. Machine learning models help detect unusual patterns.

Code for detecting anomalies in access logs:

python

```
import pandas as pd
from sklearn.ensemble import IsolationForest

df = pd.read_csv("access_logs.csv")
model = IsolationForest(contamination=0.01)
df["anomaly"] = model.fit_predict(df[["access_count",
"failed_attempts"]])

anomalies = df[df["anomaly"] == -1]
print(anomalies)
```

This code uses Isolation Forest to identify anomalous patterns in access logs, helping to detect unauthorized access.

Incident response

An incident response plan must contain actions to mitigate the impact of a breach. Key steps include:

1. **Identification and containment**: Isolate affected systems to prevent spread.
2. **Analysis of the origin of the attack**: understand how the failure occurred.
3. **Security correction and reinforcement**: Apply patches and increase controls.
4. **Communication and compliance**: notify authorities and users as required by law.

Automatic incident notification via Slack API:

python

```python
import requests

def notify_slack(message):
    webhook_url = "https://hooks.slack.com/services/YOUR/WEBHOOK/URL"
    payload = {"text": message}
    requests.post(webhook_url, json=payload)

notify_slack("Alert: possible data leak identified!")
```

This code sends an automatic notification to a channel on the Slack, enabling rapid response to incidents.

Security Frameworks for DataOps

Implementing security frameworks standardizes data protection practices and facilitates auditing and regulatory compliance.

Zero Trust Architecture

The concept of Zero Trust It is based on the principle that no entity, internal or external, should be automatically trusted. Practices include:

- **Multi-factor authentication (MFA)**: requiring multiple checks for access.

- **Network segmentation**: limiting data access to authorized users only.

- **Continuous monitoring**: Detecting suspicious activity in real time.

NIST Cybersecurity Framework

NIST (National Institute of Standards and Technology) developed a security framework that helps organizations structure their data protection strategies. It is based on five pillars:

1. **Identify**: map critical assets and associated risks.
2. **Protect**: Implement controls to reduce vulnerabilities.
3. **Detect**: Monitor events to identify threats.
4. **Responder**: define incident response plans.
5. **Recover**: Restore operations quickly after an incident.

Security Tools for DataOps

Several tools help ensure the security of data pipelines:

- **Vault (HashiCorp)**: secure credential and key management.

- **AWS KMS (Key Management Service)**: encryption key management service.

- **Azure Purview**: cataloging and data protection in the cloud.

- **Splunk**: Real-time threat monitoring and detection.

Security and privacy in DataOps require a multifaceted approach, combining encryption, monitoring, automation, and security frameworks. Regulatory compliance must be a priority, ensuring data is processed ethically and legally. By implementing robust strategies, cyber attacks and leaks can be minimized, protecting valuable assets and ensuring the reliability of data flows.

CHAPTER 17 – TRENDS AND INNOVATIONS IN DATAOPS

The evolution of DataOps follows the exponential growth in data generation and the new technologies that emerge to optimize the collection, processing and analysis processes. Artificial intelligence and automation play a central role in transforming data flows, while quantum computing promises to revolutionize the way large volumes of information are processed. The advancement of these technologies shapes the future of intelligent data pipelines, making them more efficient, autonomous and adaptable to complex scenarios.

The impact of AI and Automation on DataOps

Artificial intelligence (AI) and automation bring significant changes to DataOps, reducing the need for human intervention and making processes more agile. These technologies allow you to detect patterns, predict failures and optimize data flow based on continuous learning.

Process automation

Automation in DataOps eliminates repetitive tasks, improving data engineering efficiency. Processes such as integrating new data sources, cleaning information and monitoring pipelines can be automated.

Data cleaning automation with **Pandas**:

python

```
import pandas as pd

def clean_data(df):
    df = df.dropna() # Remove rows with null values
    df = df.drop_duplicates() # Remove duplicate values
    df.columns = [col.strip().lower() for col in df.columns]  #
Padroniza nomes das colunas
    return df

data = pd.read_csv("raw_data.csv")
cleaned_data = clean_data(data)
cleaned_data.to_csv("cleaned_data.csv", index=False)
```

This code automates the removal of inconsistencies in datasets, ensuring that only clean information is processed.

AI in anomaly detection

Machine learning models are used to identify unusual patterns in data pipelines. Anomaly detection algorithms analyze variations in information and identify potential failures or improper access.

Code for detecting anomalies in sensor data:

python

```
from sklearn.ensemble import IsolationForest
import pandas as pd

df = pd.read_csv("sensor_data.csv")
model = IsolationForest(contamination=0.02)
df["anomaly"] = model.fit_predict(df[["temperature", "pressure"]])

anomalies = df[df["anomaly"] == -1]
```

STUDIOD21 SMART TECH CONTENT

```
print(anomalies)
```

This code detects abnormal variations in temperature and pressure sensors, helping to predict failures in critical systems.

Autonomous Data Pipelines

AI allows you to create data pipelines that dynamically adapt to changes in information flows. Algorithms can identify bottlenecks, predict failures, and automatically adjust infrastructure to maintain optimal performance.

Code for automatic resource adjustment based on data traffic:

python

```python
import random

def adjust_resources(data_load):
    if data_load > 80:
        return "Increase cluster size"
    elif data_load < 30:
        return "Decrease cluster size"
    return "Keep current settings"

current_load = random.randint(10, 100)
decision = adjust_resources(current_load)
print(f"Current Load: {current_load}% - Decision: {decision}")
```

This code simulates a system that dynamically adjusts processing capacity according to demand.

How quantum computing can affect DataOps

Quantum computing offers a new paradigm for data processing, allowing us to solve problems that would be unfeasible for traditional computers. The speed and efficiency of these systems open up new possibilities for DataOps, especially in areas that require complex analysis.

Acceleration of data processing

Quantum computers use qubits to process information in parallel, providing an exponential gain in speed in certain operations. This could revolutionize the processing of large volumes of data in sectors such as healthcare, finance and scientific research.

Quantum Algorithms for DataOps

Applying quantum algorithms can optimize AI model training, improve predictive analytics, and increase the efficiency of data pipelines.

Code to generate quantum states using the library **Kiskit**:

python

```
from qiskit import QuantumCircuit, Aer, transpile, assemble, execute

qc = QuantumCircuit(2)
qc.h(0) # Apply a Hadamard gate to the first qubit
qc.cx(0, 1) # Apply a CNOT gate, creating entanglement

simulator = Aer.get_backend('statevector_simulator')
job = execute(qc, simulator)
result = job.result()
print(result.get_statevector())
```

This code creates a simple quantum circuit and displays the resulting quantum states, demonstrating one of the fundamental principles of quantum computing.

Quantum security and cryptography

Quantum computing also impacts security in DataOps. Quantum algorithms can break traditional encryption systems, but they can also create new security models based on quantum principles, such as quantum key distribution (QKD), which guarantees secure communication.

The Future of Smart Data Pipelines

The data pipelines of the future will be highly automated, intelligent and adaptable. The combination of AI, quantum computing and automation will create data streams that operate with maximum efficiency, security and scalability.

Integrating DataOps with emerging technologies

The evolution of data pipelines involves convergence with emerging technologies:

- **Edge Computing**: Decentralized processing to reduce latencies and optimize real-time analysis.

- **Blockchain**: Enhanced security in data integrity and transaction traceability.

- **AI-Driven Pipelines**: data flows managed by artificial intelligence, optimizing operations without human intervention.

Adaptable and scalable pipelines

The data pipelines of the future will be able to automatically adjust their resources based on demand. This includes:

- **Autoscaling**: dynamic allocation of computational resources to avoid bottlenecks.

- **AI-based optimization**: continuous analysis to improve process efficiency.

- **Seamless integration of multiple sources**: data coming from different systems will be automatically standardized and integrated.

Development of serverless architectures for DataOps

The architecture **serverless** eliminates the need for manual server management, allowing data pipelines to run only when needed. This reduces operating costs and increases efficiency.

Code for serverless data pipeline with **AWS Lambda**:

python

```python
import boto3

def process_data(event, context):
    s3 = boto3.client("s3")
    data = s3.get_object(Bucket="my-data-bucket", Key="data.csv")
    content = data["Body"].read().decode("utf-8")
    return f"Data processed: {len(content.splitlines())} rows"

print(process_data(None, None))
```

This code uses AWS Lambda to process files from a S3 Bucket, demonstrating how data pipelines can be optimized in serverless architectures.

DataOps is evolving rapidly with the integration of AI, quantum computing, and new processing architectures. The future of data pipelines will be defined by automation, scalability and improved security, making them more efficient and adaptable to business needs. Using these emerging technologies will enable organizations to transform large volumes of data into valuable insights faster and more accurately.

CHAPTER 18 – HOW TO IMPLEMENT DATAOPS IN YOUR COMPANY

The adoption of DataOps allows companies to optimize their data management and analysis processes, reducing operational bottlenecks and increasing team efficiency. Successful implementation involves a structured approach, from defining strategies to measuring results.

Step by step to start DataOps from scratch

Implementing DataOps requires careful planning, alignment with company objectives, and the integration of appropriate technologies. The process can be divided into fundamental steps.

Defining objectives and requirements

The first step to implementing DataOps is establishing what problems need to be solved. Some essential points include:

- **Identification of the company's needs**: understand whether the priority is to improve data quality, reduce processing times or optimize storage.

- **Mapping existing data flows**: analyze how data is collected, transformed and used.

- **Alignment with corporate strategy**: ensuring that DataOps brings value to business areas.

Choice of tools and infrastructure

Choosing the right infrastructure and tools directly impacts DataOps efficiency. Some of the most common options include:

- **Storage and processing**: databases such as PostgreSQL, MongoDB, Snowflake and distributed systems such as Apache Hadoop and Apache Spark.

- **Pipeline orchestration**: Apache Airflow, Prefect, and Dagster are popular platforms for managing data flows.

- **Monitoring and observability**: tools like Prometheus and Grafana help monitor process performance.

- **Continuous data integration**: Platforms like dbt (Data Build Tool) and Fivetran automate data transformation and ingestion.

Building the DataOps team

The DataOps team needs professionals with technical and strategic skills. Some of the essential roles include:

- **Data engineer**: Responsible for building and maintaining efficient pipelines.

- **Data scientist**: uses the processed data to create analytical and predictive models.

- **DevOps for data**: automates processes and manages scalable infrastructure.

- **Data Analyst**: Interprets information to generate actionable insights.

Building scalable data pipelines

Building efficient pipelines is one of the pillars of DataOps. The data flow must be continuous, automated and secure.

Code model for creating a basic pipeline using Apache Airflow:

python

```
from airflow import DAG
from airflow.operators.python_operator import PythonOperator
from datetime import datetime
import pandas as pd

def extract_data():
    df = pd.read_csv("data.csv")
    df.to_csv("extracted_data.csv", index=False)

def transform_data():
    df = pd.read_csv("extracted_data.csv")
    df["processed"] = df["value"] * 2 # Simple transformation
    df.to_csv("transformed_data.csv", index=False)

def load_data():
    df = pd.read_csv("transformed_data.csv")
    df.to_csv("final_data.csv", index=False)

default_args = {"start_date": datetime(2024, 1, 1)}
dag = DAG("data_pipeline", default_args=default_args,
schedule_interval="@daily")

task1 = PythonOperator(task_id="extract",
```

```
python_callable=extract_data, dag=dag)
task2 = PythonOperator(task_id="transform",
python_callable=transform_data, day=day)
task3 = PythonOperator(task_id="load",
python_callable=load_data, dag=dag)

task1 >> task2 >> task3
```

This code creates an automated workflow that extracts, transforms, and loads data in a scalable way.

Adoption checklist and main challenges

The transition to DataOps requires detailed planning to avoid failures. Some practices guarantee more efficient implementation.

Checklist for DataOps adoption

- Set goals and expectations aligned with the company's strategy.

- Choose tools compatible with the existing infrastructure.

- Structure a team with essential functions.

- Create scalable and monitorable data pipelines.

- Implement security and data access control.

- Automate processes to ensure operational efficiency.

- Develop metrics to monitor performance and data quality.

Main challenges

DataOps adoption can face obstacles that need to be overcome to ensure a successful implementation.

- **Resistance to change**: employees accustomed to traditional processes may resist the adoption of new methodologies.

- **Integration of multiple data sources**: Consolidating information from different systems can be complex.

- **Data quality assurance**: Inconsistencies, duplications, and incomplete information impact the effectiveness of pipelines.

- **Security and regulatory compliance**: Protection against unauthorized access and compliance with laws such as GDPR and LGPD are mandatory.

How to measure implementation success

DataOps efficiency must be measured to ensure continuous improvements. Some metrics help evaluate the results obtained.

Performance indicators

- **Data processing time**: measure the reduction in the time needed to collect, transform and make data available.

- **Error rate in pipelines**: Track failures in the execution of workflows.

- **Reliability and availability**: ensuring that systems operate with minimal downtime.

- **Efficient use of resources**: check whether the infrastructure is being used optimally.

Continuous monitoring

The observability of pipelines allows for proactive adjustments and ensures long-term efficiency. Tools like Prometheus and Grafana allow you to track metrics and detect anomalies quickly.

Code for monitoring a pipeline using Prometheus:

python

```python
from prometheus_client import start_http_server, Summary
import time
import random

REQUEST_TIME = Summary('data_pipeline_processing_time',
'Time spent processing data')

@REQUEST_TIME.time()
def process_data():
    time.sleep(random.uniform(0.1, 1.0))

if __name__ == "__main__":
    start_http_server(8000)
    while True:
        process_data()
```

This code launches a Prometheus server that monitors the execution time of a data pipeline, allowing bottlenecks to be identified.

Continuous feedback and optimization

DataOps success depends on continuous improvement based on

metrics and team feedback. Some strategies include:

- **Periodic performance reviews**: evaluate bottlenecks and optimization opportunities.

- **Automation Enhancement**: Reduce manual processes whenever possible.

- **Constant team training**: Ensure everyone is up to date with best practices.

The implementation of DataOps transforms the way companies deal with data, making processes more agile, efficient and scalable. A structured approach, with clear definition of objectives, choice of appropriate tools and continuous monitoring, ensures that adoption is successful. Automation, security and data quality are determining factors for obtaining consistent results and maximizing the strategic value of information.

CHAPTER 19 – SUCCESS STORIES AND LESSONS LEARNED

The adoption of DataOps has transformed the way companies deal with data, bringing operational efficiency, agility and greater quality to strategic decisions. Several organizations from different sectors have applied DataOps to optimize their processes, overcome technical challenges and achieve significant benefits.

Case studies of companies that have adopted DataOps

Technology, healthcare, finance and commerce companies have adopted DataOps to solve challenges related to data quality, pipeline automation and scalability. Analysis of real cases offers valuable insights into the benefits of implementation.

Case 1: Technology company improving data scalability

A global technology company that operates video streaming services was struggling to process large volumes of data in real time. The accelerated growth of the user base has increased the complexity of pipelines, leading to recurrent failures, high latency and difficulties in predictive analysis.

Solution applied

The company adopted DataOps to revamp its data ingestion and transformation processes. Key changes included:

- Implementation of Apache Kafka for continuous ingestion of user events.

- Use of Apache Spark for distributed real-time data processing.

- Monitoring with Prometheus and Grafana to detect performance bottlenecks.

- Pipeline automation with Apache Airflow.

Code for pipeline optimized with Kafka and Spark

python

```python
from pyspark.sql import SparkSession
from pyspark.sql.functions import col

spark = SparkSession.builder \
    .appName("StreamingPipeline") \
    .getOrCreate()

df = spark.readStream \
    .format("kafka") \
    .option("kafka.bootstrap.servers", "localhost:9092") \
    .option("subscribe", "user_events") \
    .load()

df_transformed = df.selectExpr("CAST(value AS STRING)").alias("event_data")

query = df_transformed.writeStream \
    .format("console") \
    .start()
```

```
query.awaitTermination()
```

This pipeline captures user data in real time and processes it in a scalable way.

Benefits obtained

- Reduction of data processing time from 30 minutes to less than 5 seconds.

- Improved user experience with real-time recommendations.

- Greater system stability, reducing failures and latency.

Lessons learned

- Automation dramatically reduces response time to data events.

- Scalable pipelines enable growth without compromising performance.

- Continuous monitoring prevents problems before they impact users.

Case 2: Digital banking improving data quality and security

A digital bank faced data quality challenges due to duplicate and inconsistent information across different sources. Furthermore, compliance with regulations such as LGPD and GDPR required greater control over access and process auditing.

Solution applied

The company implemented DataOps to ensure data integrity and optimize security. The strategies adopted included:

- Use of dbt (Data Build Tool) to standardize and validate data.
- Application of Data Governance with tools like Collibra from the Apache Atlas.

- Access monitoring and audit trail with AWS CloudTrail.

- Permissions control using IAM (Identity and Access Management).

Code model for data quality validation with dbt

yaml

```yaml
version: 2

models:
  - name: transactions
    description: "Table of validated financial transactions"
    columns:
      - name: transaction_id
        tests:
          - unique
          - not_null
      - name: amount
        tests:
          - not_null
          - positive_values
```

This code defines rules to prevent duplicate transactions or inconsistent values.

Benefits obtained

- Reduction of inconsistencies by 80%, ensuring more reliable data.

- Full compliance with regulations, avoiding fines and sanctions.

- Greater operational efficiency with automation of audits and reports.

Lessons learned

- Data governance is essential to maintaining quality and compliance.

- Adopting good practices reduces operational and financial risks.

- Automated validations minimize human errors and inconsistencies.

Case 3: Global retailer optimizing demand forecasts

A global retail chain was having difficulty predicting product demand in different regions. The challenge included dispersed data, poor integration between systems and failures to update reports.

Solution applied

The company implemented DataOps to improve demand predictability. Actions taken included:

- Centralization of data in one Data Lake based on AWS S3.

- Use of Automated ETL with AWS Glue to transform data in real time.

- Implementation of predictive models with TensorFlow e Pandas.

Code for demand forecasting using machine learning

python

```
import pandas as pd
from tensorflow import keras
from sklearn.model_selection import train_test_split

data = pd.read_csv("sales_data.csv")
X = data.drop(columns=["demand"])
y = data["demand"]

X_train, X_test, y_train, y_test = train_test_split(X, y,
test_size=0.2)

model =keras.Sequential([
    keras.layers.Dense(64, activation="relu"),
    keras.layers.Dense(32, activation="relu"),
    hard.layers.Dense(1)
])

model.compile(optimizer="adam", loss="mse")
model.fit(X_train, y_train, epochs=10, batch_size=32)
```

This AI model predicts product demand based on historical data.

Benefits obtained

- Forecast accuracy increased by 40%, reducing unnecessary inventories.

- Report update time reduced from 24 hours to less than 1 hour.

- Efficient integration between data, logistics and sales teams.

Lessons learned

- Pipeline automation accelerates access to strategic insights.

- Predictive models allow for more informed and assertive decisions.
- Integration between different areas improves operational efficiency.

Learnings for different sectors

The case studies show that DataOps can be applied across industries to solve specific challenges. Some general learnings include:

- **Technology**: DataOps improves scalability by ensuring efficient processing of large volumes of data.

- **Finance**: Data governance and regulatory compliance are crucial to reducing risk and maintaining information integrity.

- **Retail**: Automating demand forecasts allows for more strategic decisions and reduced operational costs.

- **Health**: Data quality and security are essential to ensure accurate diagnostics and regulatory compliance.

Adopting DataOps brings significant benefits to companies across different sectors. Scalability, automation and data governance improve operational efficiency, reducing risk and increasing the accuracy of strategic decisions. The case studies analyzed show that successful implementation requires integration of tools, continuous monitoring and an organizational culture focused on innovation.

CHAPTER 20 – THE FUTURE OF DATA-DRIVEN DECISIONS

The digital era has transformed the way companies and individuals make decisions. The exponential growth in the amount of data available, combined with technological advances such as artificial intelligence, automation and cloud computing, has created a scenario where data-based decisions are essential for competitiveness. DataOps emerges as a fundamental element in this evolution, ensuring that data is treated with quality, efficiency and reliability.

Reflection on the impact of DataOps in the digital age

The digitalization of business processes and the growing adoption of technologies such as the Internet of Things (IoT), machine learning and blockchain have increased the demand for reliable data available in real time. However, simply collecting data is not enough. The big challenge is transforming this information into actionable knowledge.

Companies that adopt DataOps gain significant strategic advantages. Among the main impacts, the following stand out:

- **Speed in decision making**: With automated pipelines and optimized infrastructure, companies reduce the time between data generation and its practical use.

- **Reduction of errors and inconsistencies**: Data governance and automated processes guarantee greater accuracy and reliability in the information analyzed.

- **Greater collaboration between teams**: DataOps promotes integration between data scientists, software engineers and managers, creating a more efficient workflow.

- **Ability to adapt to changes**: Data-driven companies can react quickly to market changes, adjusting strategies based on insights extracted in real time.

The rise of DataOps also drives the development of tools and methodologies to improve data lifecycle management. New platforms and frameworks are constantly emerging to facilitate the integration, processing and analysis of large volumes of information.

How professionals should prepare for this new reality

The demand for qualified DataOps professionals grows as companies seek to better structure their data processes. To operate in this scenario, a set of technical and strategic skills is required to ensure an in-depth understanding of data flow and best automation practices.

Essential technical skills

- **Programming languages**: Knowledge of Python and SQL is essential for data manipulation, extraction and analysis.

- **Automation and orchestration tools**: Experience with Apache Airflow, Kubernetes and Jenkins for managing data pipelines.

- **Storage and processing platforms**: Mastery of relational and non-relational databases, as well as solutions such as AWS S3, Google BigQuery and Snowflake.

- **Monitoring and observability**: Ability to implement metrics and logs in tools such as Prometheus and Grafana, ensuring the health of data pipelines.

- **Data security and governance**: Knowledge of regulatory frameworks such as GDPR and LGPD to ensure compliance and information protection.

Strategic and behavioral skills

- **Analytical thinking**: Ability to interpret patterns in data and propose innovative solutions.

- **Effective communication**: Professionals must be able to translate technical insights to business teams and vice versa.

- **Teamwork**: DataOps requires constant collaboration between different areas, making the ability to work in groups essential.

- **Continuous learning**: The technological scenario is constantly evolving, requiring frequent updates on new tools and methodologies.

The training of a DataOps professional can occur either through specialized courses or through practical experience in implementing data pipelines.

Code example for automating a data pipeline with Apache Airflow

python

```python
from airflow import DAG
from airflow.operators.python import PythonOperator
from datetime import datetime

def extract_data():
    print("Extracting data...")

def transform_data():
    print("Transforming data...")

def load_data():
    print("Loading data...")

default_args = {
    'owner': 'airflow',
    'start_date': datetime(2024, 1, 1),
    'retries': 1,
}

day = DAY(
    'data_pipeline',
    default_args=default_args,
    schedule_interval='@daily',
)

extract_task = PythonOperator(
    task_id='extract',
    python_callable=extract_data,
    day=day,
)

transform_task = PythonOperator(
    task_id='transform',
    python_callable=transform_data,
    day=day,
```

```
)

load_task = PythonOperator(
    task_id='load',
    python_callable=load_data,
    day=day,
)

extract_task >> transform_task >> load_task
```

This code defines a simple pipeline in Apache Airflow, automating the data extraction, transformation and loading steps.

Latest recommendations for companies and individuals

For DataOps to be implemented successfully and bring positive results, both companies and professionals must adopt a data-driven mindset and follow best practices.

For companies

1. **Establish a data culture**: Data-driven decision-making should be encouraged at all levels of the organization.
2. **Invest in scalable infrastructure**: Choosing appropriate tools and platforms is essential to ensure efficient data processing.
3. **Automate processes whenever possible**: Automation reduces manual errors and speeds up workflow.
4. **Continuously monitor and improve**: Analysis of operational metrics allows constant adjustments to optimize pipelines.
5. **Ensure security and compliance**: Responsible use of data avoids legal problems and strengthens users' trust.

For individuals

1. **Develop a continuous learning mindset**: Technologies evolve quickly, and staying up to date is essential to remain competitive.
2. **Practice implementing pipelines**: Practical learning is essential to consolidate technical knowledge.
3. **Search for certifications and specializations**: Certification programs can help validate skills in the job market.
4. **Improve communication and teamwork**: DataOps professionals need to collaborate with different areas to ensure the success of projects.
5. **Explore new technologies and trends**: Monitoring innovations allows adaptation and taking advantage of new opportunities.

The future of data-driven decisions will increasingly be driven by DataOps. The ability to process large volumes of information in real time, ensuring quality and reliability, will be a competitive differentiator for companies in all sectors. For individuals, the constant search for technical and strategic knowledge will be crucial to standing out in the market. By adopting DataOps in a structured and efficient way, organizations and professionals will be prepared for the challenges and opportunities of the digital era.

FINAL CONCLUSION

The evolution of technologies and the explosion in the amount of available data have made the search for agility and efficiency in information management essential. DataOps emerges as an indispensable approach for companies that want to transform raw data into strategic insights quickly and with quality. Effective DataOps implementation enables reliable data flows, promotes integration between teams, and ensures scalability to meet the demands of modern businesses.

The concept of DataOps was explored from its definition to its practical application in various sectors. Below is a summary of the main lessons covered:

Chapter 1 – What is DataOps?
DataOps is a methodology that combines DevOps principles, data governance, and automation to optimize the data lifecycle. Its origin lies in the need to process large volumes of information in an agile and reliable manner. Compared to DevOps and MLOps, DataOps focuses on the efficiency of data flow. Companies that adopt this approach improve the speed and quality of decision making.

Chapter 2 – DataOps Principles
DataOps is based on process automation, cross-team collaboration, and implementing strict governance. Data management must guarantee quality, security and observability, allowing information to be processed and delivered flawlessly.

Chapter 3 – DataOps Architecture

The DataOps framework includes data pipelines, stream orchestration, and continuous monitoring. The choice between on-premise or cloud infrastructure impacts scalability and efficiency. Tools such as Apache Airflow, Kubernetes and Snowflake are essential in implementation.

Chapter 4 – DataOps Culture and Mindset

Companies must encourage a culture of collaboration and an agile mindset, promoting the integration of data scientists, engineers and business analysts. The elimination of organizational silos and the adoption of iterative methodologies guarantee an efficient environment.

Chapter 5 – Building Agile Data Pipelines

Data flow automation reduces errors and speeds delivery of insights. Efficient ETL/ELT processes ensure clean data ready for analysis, while continuous monitoring allows for quick adjustments in the face of failures.

Chapter 6 – DataOps and Cloud Computing

Cloud computing offers scalability and flexibility for DataOps. Providers such as AWS, Azure and GCP provide tools for distributed processing and cost optimization, making pipelines more robust.

Chapter 7 – Data Quality and Governance

Data reliability depends on good governance practices, compliance policies, and automated validation processes. Companies must implement mechanisms for detecting and correcting inconsistencies to avoid decisions based on erroneous information.

Chapter 8 – Automation and Continuous Integration (CI/CD) for Data

Using continuous integration pipelines ensures that data goes through automated testing before it is made available. Tools like dbt and Jenkins help in efficiently implementing CI/CD for DataOps.

Chapter 9 – Observability and Data Monitoring

Traceability of data flows is essential to identify failures and optimize performance. The implementation of dashboards and metrics enables real-time monitoring and rapid resolution of incidents.

Chapter 10 – DataOps for Business Intelligence (BI)

Reports and dashboards gain efficiency when driven by DataOps. Automation in data ingestion and transformation reduces the time required for analysis, ensuring updated and accurate insights for decision making.

Capítulo 11 – DataOps no Big Data e Machine Learning

The combination of DataOps and Machine Learning facilitates the automation of the lifecycle of predictive models. Specialized tools help manage large-scale data and improve algorithm performance.

Chapter 12 – DataOps in Finance and Banking

Security and compliance are critical for financial institutions. DataOps helps reduce fraud, optimize transactions and comply with regulations such as GDPR and LGPD.

Chapter 13 – DataOps in E-commerce and Marketing

E-commerce companies use DataOps for customer segmentation, campaign personalization and demand forecasting. Real-time analysis allows for strategic adjustments and increased sales conversion.

Chapter 14 – DataOps for Healthcare and Biotechnology
The healthcare sector benefits from the integration of clinical, genomic and laboratory data to improve diagnostics and research. However, strict regulations require greater control over data privacy and security.

Chapter 15 – Strategies for DataOps Teams
The formation of multidisciplinary teams is essential for the success of DataOps. Engineers, analysts and DevOps specialists must work together, using collaborative tools to ensure productivity.

Chapter 16 – Security and Privacy in DataOps
Protecting sensitive data is one of the biggest challenges. Companies must implement strict protocols to prevent leaks and cyberattacks, ensuring compliance with privacy regulations.

Chapter 17 – Trends and Innovations in DataOps
The advancement of artificial intelligence and automation is reshaping DataOps. Quantum computing and new data architectures promise to transform the way information is processed and analyzed.

Chapter 18 – How to Implement DataOps in Your Company
Adopting DataOps requires planning and structuring. Companies must follow a step-by-step implementation process, facing challenges such as resistance to change and lack of team qualifications.

Chapter 19 – Success Stories and Lessons Learned
Companies that implemented DataOps achieved significant gains in efficiency and innovation. The challenges overcome offer valuable insights for different sectors, showing the applicability of the methodology.

Chapter 20 – The Future of Data-Driven Decisions
DataOps will continue to evolve, driving decision-making based on real-time data. Professionals must prepare for this new reality by adopting a continuous learning mindset and exploring new technologies.

Final Message

DataOps is not just a set of tools and processes, but a fundamental change in the way data is handled. Its effective implementation transforms businesses, improves operational efficiency and strengthens competitiveness in the digital market. Companies that adopt DataOps guarantee greater quality of information and greater agility in making strategic decisions.

We appreciate your dedication throughout this guide and we hope that the knowledge acquired here can be applied in a practical and effective way. Strategic use of DataOps has the potential to revolutionize the way data is used, opening up new opportunities for innovation and growth.

Cordially,
Diego Rodrigues & Team!

www.ingramcontent.com/pod-product-compliance
Lightning Source LLC
La Vergne TN
LVHW051242050326
832903LV00028B/2530